Heba Kamal Chami, a Lebanese author with different educational backgrounds, has worked in different regions of the world. She wrote this book as a refreshing departure from current preoccupations in education, and its main aim is to show educators new and profound ways to teach and lead schools.

It can be a resource for all those who are working in education, aiming to dip their toes into educational research and reflection. A teacher plays a crucial role in shaping the lives of young people. They inspire, motivate, and encourage a new generation of learners and guide them to make a positive impact in the world around them. The author thought of writing this book as a refreshing and inspiring way for them to rethink education.

I dedicate this book to my brother Fouad Kamal Chami, who never ceases to bring joy and love into my life. Having you as a brother and close friend makes me feel incredibly fortunate. You support me like a sturdy pillar. It means a lot that you honestly want what is best for us. I am aware of the strain that comes with having so many responsibilities, yet you handled it so beautifully.

To my mother, Ikbal Yousef Azbah, my mother – a smart woman and a selfless caregiver. The person who accepts me despite my shortcomings. It inspires me how you can handle any issue tactically. I hope to have your level of wisdom.

Heba Chami

REFRAMING EDUCATION

AUSTIN MACAULEY PUBLISHERS™
LONDON • CAMBRIDGE • NEW YORK • SHARJAH

Copyright © Heba Chami 2024

The right of Heba Chami to be identified as author of this work has been asserted by the author in accordance with Federal Law No. (7) of UAE, Year 2002, Concerning Copyrights and Neighboring Rights.

All rights reserved. No part of this publication may be reproduced, stored in a retrieval system, or transmitted in any form or by any means, electronic, mechanical, photocopying, recording, or otherwise, without the prior permission of the publishers.

Any person who commits any unauthorized act in relation to this publication may be liable to legal prosecution and civil claims for damages.

The age group that matches the content of the books has been classified according to the age classification system issued by the Ministry of Culture and Youth.

ISBN – 9789948770077 – (Paperback)
ISBN – 9789948770084 – (E-Book)

Application Number: MC-10-01-1288545
Age Classification: E

Printer Name: iPrint Global Ltd
Printer Address: Witchford, England

First Published 2024
AUSTIN MACAULEY PUBLISHERS FZE
Sharjah Publishing City
P.O Box [519201]
Sharjah, UAE
www.austinmacauley.ae
+971 655 95 20

I didn't expect the first book to be as challenging and rewarding as it is. Sincerely speaking, it would not have been possible without my closest friend Amira Al Masry. A genuine and upright healthy person who inspires others by encouraging them. It's unusual to run into wonderful people like you who are intelligent and have an uncanny ability to influence people to move toward a goal.

To Mrs. Rabab Lawati, your leadership has been crucial to my development on both a professional and personal level. In my dark and terrible years, your humanity enabled me to succeed in my job. I appreciate your understanding of cultural distinctions and respect for our racial, religious, and cultural diversity.

Gratitude to Dr. Sanaa Chehayeb for your guidance throughout the research. You are special because of your patience and full support to your students. You set the bar high for emotional intelligence in leadership.

Also a special thank you to my role model, Dr. Noha Ghosseini. You have always gone above and beyond a great professor.

Furthermore, I would want to congratulate Fatma Moosa Lawati, a great lady who is incredibly inspirational. The world needs more sympathetic, kind, and eager people like you to lend a hand. To Hadi, my dearest brother, you didn't just support us when we needed you; but also used our struggles to inspire us to make changes. Your ongoing help is greatly appreciated.

To my youngest brother and soul mate Farouk, you have my eternal gratitude for the priceless counsel which you provided, and inspired me to keep going. Thank you for always being there for me through my highs and lows, and for all the love and support you have given me thus far. You being in my life is a blessing to me.

Table of Contents

Chapter 1: Children Pain	**13**
Chapter 2: Colorful Curriculums	**31**
Chapter 3: Teacher Leader	**56**
Chapter 4: Assessment and Evaluation	**90**
Chapter 5: Assignments	**112**
Chapter 6: Emotional and Social Intelligence	**117**
Chapter 7: Different Hats a Teacher Should Wear	**134**

Overview

We are in a new global economy, which requires students to acquire certain skills to face its challenges. Unfortunately, the educational systems seem to be falling behind in recognizing the effects of this new environment, which emphasizes the need to update their systems. The adoption of technology into everyday life has changed the way we do our everyday tasks. Students who are enrolled currently in school may find themselves passing the exams but unable to participate in real-life problems because they did not acquire the skills needed to succeed. The educational demands of this new century need a different way of thinking, teaching, and learning using technology. This kind of learning cannot be achieved without the alteration of teachers' instructional practices with the aim of enhancing students' skills and competencies in analyzing, interpreting, and creating knowledge, not only memorizing the content.

Education has emerged as a basic human need in today's hypercompetitive society, on par with clothing, food, and shelter. It gives us the ability to solve every issue and encourages ethical behavior and raises people's awareness of social concerns like terrorism and corruption. It can be easy to lose sight of the students, who are the most crucial reason we teach, when the responsibilities of the job become too great. Every student needs to be recognized for their special qualities because they are extraordinary. With this outlook, educators lead by example and do their part to support their institutions.

Chapter 1
Children Pain

Pain is one of the most misunderstood, underdiagnosed, and under treated/untreated medical problems, principally in children. Pain is truly both a physical and an emotional experience perceived and handled by the brain; it is a real health problem as well. Each child has a different pain perception, and the meaning of pain is also different from child to child.

In addition to being a location for learning, schools frequently put and modify your child's social life and athletic activities. It's crucial that we assist our pupils in developing reasonable expectations for what they can do in terms of their academic endeavors. Our goal as educators is to educate these kids, not just help them get good scores or finish up any unfinished work. Teachers mentor students and assist them in learning how to pace their academic work. Putting effort into your pupils as a teacher develops relationships with them and makes them feel valued. A pupil responds to a teacher who shows concern and feels more at ease to contribute.

When the teacher engages in meaningful communication with them and shows genuine interest in them, they feel better. The fact that students unavoidably run across issues that inhibit or hinder their full and effective participation in the study process necessitates the need for various adjustments throughout the study process and in the study environment. However, children's learning styles vary, and they frequently feel as though they are falling short in particular areas.

As a result of the challenges they inevitably face that impede or hinder them from participating fully and effectively in the study process, students need various adjustments both during the study process and in the study environment. However, because every child learns differently, they frequently feel like they are failing in some subjects. Teachers, on the other hand, can substantially assist them by designing classes for students of various levels and taking into account each student's unique qualities. You can learn about the role of the teacher in assisting a student in reaching success by reading through various instances that actually occurred in this chapter.

On the other hand, teachers may substantially aid them by designing classes for various learning styles and taking into account each student's unique strengths. This chapter will give you access to a number of real-life examples and explain how teachers may help students achieve their goals.

Gilbert's Story

"A good teacher should be able to put himself in the place of those who find learning hard."

Elphas Levi

Background

Gilbert is a young student who had aggressive and daredevil behavior. He is always unorganized and unwilling to learn. He has been struggling academically for different reasons since middle school. He was retained in sixth grade and was two to three years behind grade level in different parts and skills.

During his early school years, he had problems with concentration, which prevented him from completing assignments on time and from meeting responsibilities. He received much criticism from his teachers and friends and nobody tried to find out the reasons behind this.

Gilbert lives with his mom and stepdad. His biological parents divorced when he was entering third grade, and he and his mom went to live with his grandparents. His mom married his stepdad when he entered the sixth grade. The school counselor met with Gilbert and his mom that year to address his academic and behavioral problems. It was determined that he was "having difficulty" adjusting to all the changes in his life, particularly having a new person striving for his mom's attention. Gilbert unfortunately considers himself an unwanted and unworthy person.

Family Interactions

- Gilbert's parents have been contacted by phone but have been unable to leave work to attend all the conferences.
- They have expressed dissatisfaction with the school for the way their son has been treated; in their view, teachers pick on him and are too quick to blame him for minor offenses.
- He was suspended many times because he found it hard not to bother his friends in different ways. Even at home, he has difficulties with his sister. He pulls her hair, pinches her cheek, and breaks her toys.
- He doesn't know how to express what he wants; he uses his hands or shouts instead of communicating with people. He had difficulty keeping his hands to himself, often displaying aggressive and impulsive behavior.

Understanding

Never forget that no two kids are alike and that there is no such thing as a 'one size fits all' approach. Various brains exist. Gilbert was subsequently identified as an ADD student. Many teachers wrongly believe that children with ADD are spoilt, rude, or that they come from dysfunctional households where their parents don't love them. This method of blaming parents is the first step in the wrong direction when trying to diagnose an issue. Not all parents are educated, and even those who are sometimes have no clue about education or pupils with special needs unless they work in this field. Most ADD students are impulsive and overactive. They frequently take action without first considering the effects of their choices.

The education community consists of some of the most highly trained people in the world. So why are we educators so inexperienced at improving student academic performance? Between symptoms and causes, educators need to explore the roots of the problem and dig into the origins of learners' academic tortures. Instructors should be excellent diagnosticians in order to achieve this. They must examine the situation and determine—or diagnose—the source of a student's learning problem.

Some of the world's most skilled professionals work in the field of education. Why then are we teachers so ineffective in raising students' academic performance?

Between the causes and the effects. Teachers must look into the causes of the issue and the beginnings of students' academic torments. To do this, instructors need be skilled diagnosticians. They need to assess the issue and identify or, more precisely, diagnose the cause of a student's learning difficulty. An incorrect diagnosis may result in surface alterations and brief performance gains, but it won't fully resolve the problem. Educators must continue to work their way toward the source and refrain from offering rash advice. Educators must stay the course toward the source, however, and not make hasty recommendations. An improper diagnosis may produce superficial changes and temporary performance improvements, but it won't fully cure the issue.

Incorrect diagnoses aren't limited to the education field. Consider medicine, for example. Doctors once used a variety of treatment methods for people who testified severe leg pain. These remedies provided temporary relief but never fully alleviated the pain or allowed patients to regain their pre-condition quality of life. It wasn't until the medical community realized that the pain's source was the sciatic nerve, which originates in the lower spine, not the leg. In a condition called referred pain, a patient's discomfort manifests at a place different from its source. Understanding this has enabled physicians to develop the correct responses to sciatica. Now, in most cases, they can actually solve the problem, and patients can regain their normal quality of life.

I've been privileged to work with lots of education institutions and high schools. I believe many educators are responding to an academic form of referred pain, whereby they're treating various manifestations of student problems rather than the actual sources. I'm convinced that just as proper diagnoses lead to effective treatments of physical ailments, pinpointing the reason(s) that a student's learning has short-circuited—that he or she is frustrated, apathetic, underperforming, missing class, or even considering withdrawing from school—can help educators dramatically improve student learning, attitude, and performance. The challenge is identifying the source. At their core, student problems are dispositional, conceptual, skill-based, or a combination of these. The problem may not be out of willingness; it could be a mental health problem in students, which includes several types of emotional and behavioral disorders, including disruptive behavior, depression, anxiety, or even autism. Childhood mental health disorders have significant negative impacts on the individual, the family, and society. It is particularly important for all teachers to be aware of the real reasons why students are academically struggling to succeed or their misbehavior. Teachers have to know the importance of their job and have to diagnose just like doctors. Even if they are not psychiatric, they should have an idea about the childhood psychology, mental problems, and how to deal with these children because their pain is inside, and sometimes even some words can be painful to them.

Mental health disorders are very common in childhood, and they include emotional-obsessive-compulsive disorder, anxiety, depression, conduct disorder (CD), attention deficit hyperactivity disorder (ADHD), developmental (speech/language delay, intellectual disability) disorders, or pervasive (autistic spectrum) disorders. While low-intensity naughty, defiant, and impulsive behavior from time to time, losing one's temper, destruction of property, and dishonesty /stealing in preschool children are regarded as normal, extremely difficult and challenging behaviors outside the norm for the age and level of development, such as unpredictable, prolonged, and/or destructive tantrums and severe outbursts of temper loss are recognized as behavior disorders.

Hadi Story

"One looks back with appreciation to the brilliant teachers, but with gratitude to those who touched our human feelings. The curriculum is so much necessary raw material, but warmth is the vital element for the growing plant and for the soul of the child."

Carl Jung

Background

Hadi was perceived as a student who struggled in the classroom. He was considered as the 'black sheep' of the group. He was continuously criticized and punished, which caused him to have a negative self-image and lack of confidence for the rest of his life.

Family Interaction:

- His astonishing failure signified nothing more than that he doesn't pay close attention to details or makes thoughtless blunders in homework; the problem was never identified by the school.

- Hadi was most of the time absent for different untrue excuses.
- Hadi's teachers frequently voiced their displeasure with his performance, but his parents were unable to attend meetings and his mother refused to inform his father about him.

A teacher has to know that every student is unique and that no student should be left behind. Students become disruptive when their class is boring and not interactive, or when they feel they are left aside and not part of the lesson. They also try to make different excuses just to skip classes.

The student may lag behind in their academics, lose their spot on a team, and miss out on social developments when they are not involved or respected. He/she may find it more challenging to resume their studies and the numerous social activities that revolve around school the longer it takes for them to return to class. Some kids may reject attempts to get them back into class because they are relieved to be out of the monotony of school.

Absenteeism is a way for the student to get out of the environment that he/she couldn't belong and made him/her feel down. As Hadi did, he was always searching for a reason to be absent. A long absence from school creates disruption in all these areas. The longer it takes to return to school, the more difficult it may be for your child to return to their studies and the other social activities that revolve around school. Some children are pleased to be out of the drudgery of school and may resist attempts to get them back into class.

When a student doesn't do well in school, educators logically conclude that the student lacks the necessary skills to perform the task. It's rare that a skill deficit is the sole reason for academic troubles. In other words, students have different abilities and different talents. Such was the case with Hadi; he was spending seven hours each day studying different subjects to get a grade. Hadi was not terrible but was not able to get into the system. Hadi loved to work with his hands, and he was good at math, but nobody was there to help him study history, English, biology and even languages. His parents weren't educated, and his father had a bad temper. He was always afraid to answer, even if he knew the answer. He had depression and anxiety, but nobody noticed until he left school.

Hadi's mental problem was not noticed, and his teachers blamed him without observing to determine whether he needed help or not. They just labeled him and put him down; they saw him as unskilled for a university. Hadi's failure didn't only disrupt his plans, but it devastated the entire family, and his father sent a cutting message: "If he can't make it, then none of his brothers can."

Untreated mental health problems can disrupt children's functioning at home, school, and in the community. Without treatment, children with mental health issues are at increased risk of school failure, contact with the criminal justice system, dependence on social services, and even suicide.

The following signs may indicate the need for professional help:

- Decline in school performance
- Poor grades despite strong efforts
- Constant worry or anxiety
- Absenteeism or not taking part in normal activities

- Hyperactivity
- Persistent nightmares
- Persistent disobedience or aggression
- Frequent temper tantrums
- Depression, sadness, or anxiety

Teachers should keep in mind that one size does not fit all. We are all born with diverse abilities.

1. Some students may be concerned about classroom subject matter and seek out challenging course work, participate enthusiastically in class discussions, and earn high marks on given projects.
2. Other students may be more attracted to the social side of school, interacting with classmates frequently and attending extracurricular activities almost every day.
3. Others may be focused on athletics, shining in physical education classes and playing or watching sports most afternoons and weekends.
4. Yet other students—perhaps because of a hidden learning disability, a shy character, or a seemingly clumsy body—may be motivated to avoid academics, social situations, or athletic activities.

Fundamentally, it is helpful as a teacher to think about how you would react to a situation before you actually encounter it. You can also discuss the situations with colleagues to figure out new ways of handling the problem. The teacher's preparedness to reach beyond the four walls of the classroom and faith in every child's ability to succeed inspires their students to believe in themselves and struggle for ambitious goals. Sometimes we don't need knowledge to solve a problem; we just need to be human, feel with these children, and consider their problems our problems. The only thing that makes us unsubstituted with robots is that we have empathy. Teachers should be looking for ways to inspire students in all aspects of their lives, and for many teachers, their greatest goal is to be a role model. A role model is someone who inspires and encourages students to struggle for greatness and teaches them through experience and commitment how to realize their full potential to become the best they can be. Teachers can inspire an uninterested student to become enthralled in learning and motivated to participate. They can even bring introverted students out of their shells. A great teacher can get students reading, inspire a passion for languages, make math or science fun, and turn history lessons into exciting stories. So often, we hear people say that they were inspired to pursue their careers because of their teachers. A great teacher can leave an enduring mark that lasts a lifetime, and for many of us, some of our most important decisions were inspired by our teachers. For instance, John Hopkins was inspired by his teacher.

Aram story

"We need to give each other the space to grow, to be ourselves, and to exercise our diversity. We need to give each other space so that we may both give and receive such beautiful things as ideas, openness, dignity, joy, healing, and inclusion."

Max de Pere

Background

Aram is a student with dark skin who is educated, comes from a good family, and may be regarded as the ideal child for any parent. Aram received distinct treatment merely because of his race. The issue is that he was bullied, and the teachers were out sight-seeing without giving any importance to how he felt about what was happening among the kids. Aram's grades began to slip, and he was left alone in class until his teacher assigned him a chore.

Family Interactions

- Parents were complaining about students dealing with Aram.
- His family considered him their golden child. To them, he was the one who would make it to college. They consider the school is responsible for his failure and started thinking about changing school.
- The school considered that it cannot change the mindset of the students, and his parents should help him understand them so as not to be affected by the environment.

Some student challenges are dispositional in nature. Learners may not even be aware that their mindset regarding learning environments or a particular learning situation influences them to failure. Children have the right to talk to their own language, their own culture. We must fight the cultural authority and fight the system by allowing the children to express themselves in their own way. It is not the children who ought to change, but the system of the school where all children are recognized, respected, and appreciated for themselves. I believe diversity and equity is a need in every school. Ambitious teachers are the ones who enter this career to affect change. They make it their goal to help improve the quality of education for everyone. When a teacher says his/her goal is to 'make a difference', this is what they mean. They not only want to change the lives of their students; they want to change the face of education. Teachers also learn a great deal about themselves through teaching. Teaching requires you to step out of yourself in a way you may have never done before, and through this, you learn about yourself as a teacher and as a person. You may learn more about how you work with others, particularly with children, and better understand how to communicate effectively and teach efficiently. Furthermore, many teachers say the lessons they learn from their own students are the ones that make the job so fulfilling. Students bring a lot of their own life experiences to the classroom, and some of the things they have to say will enlighten you in ways you might not expect. They must learn about the brilliance the students bring with them "in their blood and genes." If we are to successfully educate all of our children, we must work to remove the blinders built of stereotypes, mono cultural instructional methodologies, ignorance, social distance, biased research, and racism. We must work hard to destroy those blinders so that it is possible to really see and really know the students we must teach. I pray for all of us to have the strength to teach our students what they must learn and the modesty and wisdom to learn from them so that we can better teach.

I've worked directly with schools across Oman, Lebanon, and Africa, and via online events with institutions throughout the world. Educators everywhere have shared similar experiences of how they've used insights, strategies, and tools to make immediate and, often times, remarkable improvements in student learning and performance, but as I observed, many students were left behind.

My reason for sharing these stories is to encourage educators' instincts that students can, indeed, learn more effectively and enjoy greater success. However, like the medical profession's realization that the source of unbearable leg pain could be in the lower back, we must accurately diagnose the source of learning problems.

Contrarily, reframing involves being aware of alternative readings of events and choosing the ones that produce the best results. Actually, most of the time, instead of reacting to what children do, we react to the name we give it. These names are frequently arbitrary and based on our opinions; we can never be sure which name is the right one. We are, therefore, free to select any name that produces the best result. Is a student who maintains his position considered to be 'resolute' if he is unbending? Is he 'stubborn and out to get me' or what? Which interpretation enables communication with the pupil and results in a resolution of the problem?

Look at this scenario and how it can be framed differently.

You just changed your lesson plans to incorporate small team tasks completed in class, and now you see that Joelle is leaning against her desk as her classmates work through the issue in groups. Upon being questioned about whether something is off, she responds that group projects are a 'waste of time' and that 'teachers should actually teach during class', which interaction produces the best results?

Teacher 1: frames the student as reckless: Raise your head; it's time for you to learn some responsibility.

Teacher 2: Frames it that the student needs encouragement and says to the student, "I'm glad that you like to listen to me and want me to teach, but I also believe that you are a little teacher and you can help the group." We can go over the value of group projects later.

Notice that in both cases, the student must participate, so even when we reframe the situation, as Teacher 2 did, we still aren't letting students get away with unsuitable behavior or tricking us to reduce the consequence for it. We should be friendly but firm. De-scale rather than defensive (Listen first. Speak softly).

Even when we reframe the circumstance as Teacher 2 did, we are not allowing pupils to engage in inappropriate behavior or deceiving us into reducing the consequences for it. We ought to be cordial but resolute. Rather than being defensive, listen first. Speak quietly.

This particular illustration serves as a particularly potent illustration of what reframing may accomplish. The best teachers are those who can choose the course of action that will yield the best outcome. This requires practice, the ability to look beyond the obvious, and a tremendous deal of guts to confront the issue.

How have you used reframing in your classroom, and what is the impact you've seen?

Chapter 2
Colorful Curriculums

Bamboo Curriculum

"Education is what remains after one has forgotten everything one learned in school."

– Albert Einstein

Curriculum is as an organized framework that contains the skills and content that children need to learn. As a matter of fact, we need a curriculum that doesn't change once every ten years. We need it like a bamboo, flexible and goes with the students' needs. It has many colors; blue, green, red, white, and yellow.

Bamboo curriculum is just like the bamboo plant: flexible and maybe trained to grow in unconventional shapes, and after harvest, it may be bent and utilized in different shapes according to the need. Bamboo curriculum is made of different colors and each color represents a side to focus on.

Green color means greening the curriculum; ensuring that students are capable of taking on the 21st century challenges of global warming and climate change (the most serious threat ever to face humanity), social inequities, unsustainable lifestyles, and the urgent need to switch to a renewable energy-based economy. We need a curriculum that teaches the students how to face the problems of the 21st century, especially environmental problems.

The green color represents breadth and depth of new ways to cover mandated learning outcomes while increasingly placing learning about nature, the earth, environmental solutions, and sustainable development at the heart of our teaching.

The curriculum should boost a greater understanding of the environment and ecological issues. Students should be able to practice what they learned by creating their own growing spaces, observing them, recording their hands-on research, and writing reports. Different teaching strategies can be applied to train students how to take care of their environment and keep it a safe place for them and for the new generation.

The red color represents creativity and integrating of subjects. The creativity thread integrates research, design, and optimization tools throughout the undergraduate experience.

Red color represents the part that will allow students to look behind and see the real-world applications and potential breakthroughs of the future by showing them the impact of research. For instance, exposing students to design at every level of the undergraduate experience allows them to experience the excitement of engineering by applying their foundational knowledge to a tangible product. It helps students understand why they are learning the material and how it will help them engineer a better world.

The blue color represents the side that should focus on digital literacy of students through implementing technologies into the curriculum and considering it a part of learning.

The white color is concerned with activities that endorse the knowledge, skills, and attitudes that will help people either to prevent the occurrence of conflict, resolve conflict peacefully, or create social conditions encouraging to peace. The core values of nonviolence and social justice are central to peace education. Different teaching strategies can be used, especially through the arts and sports, even through writing and other materials.

Peace Education

- Peace lessons can be introduced in a way that makes the class the most pleasant for the pupils.
- Conflict resolution topics can be applied, especially among the schoolchildren with low grades and those with "bad behavior."
- Pupils who usually do not participate in class discussions can take part in them, express their own opinions, and make comments and recommendations.
- Helps to develop analytical thinking among children.
- Leads to positive changes not only in terms of the pupils' behavior but also in their academic progress.
- Apologizing became easier, even for the most conflicting children.
- PEACE EDUCATION contributes to the improvement of pupil-parent-teacher relationships.
- Pupils should be able to independently manage and resolve everyday conflicts without the intervention of their teachers, parents, or friends, etc.

The yellow color is concerned with the moral education. It is one that works on the character and personality of the student. Ethics and values are always the main aim of education.

Students should take part in moral development exercises. There are many strategies to use. It can be taught through engaging and creative sessions, such as morning meetings, rather than being taught like science or arithmetic. This is a highly interesting problem because of the extent of student involvement and discussion. Schools are able to plan expert-led roundtable sessions.

"The Chami Bamboo Curriculum: Cultivating Knowledge and Growth"

It is extremely difficult for teachers who have been in the classroom for such a long time to persuade them that they were mistaken; it is even pointless to discuss topics with them about which they are adamant. Children's sufferings are revealed within the school's walls. This suffering manifests itself in a variety of ways, including racism, injustice, equality, and other sorts of preoccupation. Teaching our kids how to lead and understand that achieving educational justice and excellence will involve many different steps.

Children's pain tells the stories behind the walls of the school.

We all know that progress is only possible if each of us works effectively across lines of difference with students' parents and partners. Leadership is the key to transforming schools, systems, and eventually children's futures. A good school system is demanded to ensure all children are able to fulfill their potential.

Students that use our curriculum provide us feedback on how well it is working in the classroom and how we can improve. Improvement doesn't necessarily mean establishing a new school, using new technologies, or renovating a few classrooms, but rather it refers to the curriculum that pupils will be exposed to. It should balance prevocational and academic studies, enhance students' enrichment and fulfillment, and enable students to make decisions based on their talents that have an impact on the direction and quality of their entire life.

Being a professional at a job is more important than the job itself. While we are working hard to help children meet standards, remember that it is important to help them love learning and understand how to apply all the skills and knowledge to their lives. Do not isolate them from their environment. The curriculum is built, planned, designed, and constructed. It is improved, revised, and evaluated according to students' needs.

The philosophy of a school should always be the outcome of collaboration between educators, administrators, and, ideally, parents and students. Workers in the curriculum should take the time to explore their own beliefs and to articulate them based on students' needs and preferences. Education is the food for our brains and should be adapted to match children's requirements in their age.

Accordingly, since our schools are the builders of the future's minds, the need for a new curriculum is necessary; the need to implement a transferable curriculum and integrating the curriculum can be considered a step toward a new approach to learning. There is a need for an integrated curriculum that allows critical reasoning, communication, and collaboration.

Curriculum integration not only offers support that inspires children to apply skills, but it also helps students learn in a way that involves them. Many students get bored when they study math, chemistry, and other subjects from books. Curriculum integration helps avoid boring lectures and reading by showing students that what they learn has importance in the world, which is certainly not a new educational philosophy. "That value could come from using math and chemistry to create a scale model of a volcano that will motivate students when it blasts, or it could come from using geometry and woodworking skills to make a useful household item. Correlation may be as slight as casual attention to related materials in other subject areas, but it can be a bit more intense when teachers plan it to make the materials of one subject interpret the problems or topics of another. Integration is the merger of all subjects and experiences. Integrated curriculum is defined through three approaches to integration: multidisciplinary, interdisciplinary, and trans-disciplinary.

The following research I have done at my university shows the importance of applying such a curriculum in our school. Both integrated curriculum and transferable curriculum should be implemented in our schools.

Teaching Transferable Skills to Undergraduate Students

Introduction

Providing academic excellence in teaching is an essential part of any degree course. Increasingly, though, employers are looking for more than just in-depth knowledge and understanding of relevant subject material from their recruits. It is argued that part of this change has been driven by 'cuts in funding leading to higher education being more directly at the mercy of government policy' and that the employer in turn has influenced their demands. Numerous white papers and reports have impacted significantly upon higher education by highlighting the need for undergraduates to be better prepared for the world of work. To achieve the adaptability required for working within different contexts and situations, graduates are now expected to have acquired some degree of competence in a range of transferable skills to enhance their personal development and professional abilities. To meet this demand, students will be required, as part of their course, to demonstrate their communication and team-working abilities on more than one occasion; this is in addition to the more technical skills required of their disciplines.

Transferable Skills in Higher Education

It is important to recognize what has prompted the changes in higher education to accommodate the development of transferable skills. Transferable skills are not addressed seriously enough in higher education, and it is argued that course structure and delivery methods need to be radically rethought for the skills agenda to be sufficiently tackled. The reports cited a number of recommendations that were made to the government to improve the quality of higher education and included:

1. More involvement between their student populations, industry, and commerce
2. Developing program specifications that give outcomes in terms of key skills

Such government-produced publications imply the responsibility for the development of skills lies within higher education. It is also further suggested in the literature that universities and colleges should provide their students with certain skills and abilities that are applicable outside of the curriculum.

Employers are also keen for graduates to have developed their awareness and aptitude for transferable skills within higher education. Studies conducted into transferable skills in industry demonstrate the increasing pressure placed on graduates to be able to demonstrate such skills by potential employers. They echoed this view by stating that studies of employer needs have repeatedly stressed the priority, which they give to personal transferable skills. There is evidence to suggest that employers and government organizations are actively assisting higher education in this quest.

Defining Transferable Skills

It has been suggested that "transferable skills" are defined as those which are developed within education and are useful when transferred into another employment; this term is common parlance within education. The definition, however, is rather broad as it also accommodates technical skills; a more specific definition is required to differentiate between transferable and technical skills. Transferable skills have also been described as those that are needed in any job and which enable people to participate in a flexible and adaptable workforce.

Even though transferable skills can be defined in a number of ways, they are essentially job-related skills but not job-specific ones, for example, in problem solving and project management. One of the most comprehensive definitions is that provided by the Department for Skills and Education, who identify transferable skills as "those cognitive and interpersonal skills (application of number, communication, information technology, problem solving, personal skills, working with others, and improving own learning and performance) which are central to occupational competence in all sectors and at all levels." Hence, this definition is used in this paper for conceptualizing transferable skills.

Teaching approaches used to develop skills

There are several teaching approaches used to achieve the development of transferable skills in undergraduates; for the purpose of this work, three approaches are considered, 'embedding', 'integrating' and 'bolting-on' skill components. These are defined as clearly identified teaching aims and objectives relating to skills development, in which:

- **Inserting**—no direct reference is made to skills development within a module or group of modules, promoting the development of technical 'know-how'.
- **Integrating**—skills are developed in parallel with the core discipline, and the same amount of emphasis is placed on the development of transferable skills as technical abilities.
- **Bolting-on**—skills are developed independently of the core discipline enabling the explicit development of students' transferable skills.

Embedding skills into the curriculum is seen as advantageous as they forge learning links and develop a broad range of skills. It is argued that although embedded approaches have a number of intrinsic advantages, they have been difficult to operationalize effectively. It is further suggested that unless there is explicit awareness related to developing transferable skills, the associated teaching is less effective.

Bolt-on skills development (or stand-alone, as it has been re-defined) is viewed as advantageous in making skills development explicit, though students fail to grasp the academic value of such an approach.

Supports this view, maintaining, "Learning development and skills enhancement do not thrive if they are divorced from the students' overall teaching and learning experience." It is also argued that skills cannot be effectively taught in a vacuum and that skills development needs to be discipline-oriented.

There is greater support for the integration of skills into the curriculum, especially if skills are integrated into regular coursework and taught by the subject teacher. It is argued that if the provision of skill development is to incorporate knowledge and understanding, analysis, creativity, and evaluation, then integration of skills is the only viable option. Research also suggests that the integration of skill components into curricula is seen as a more effective teaching approach in higher education as it is more representative of the 'real-life' application of skills in the workplace.

This paper presents some of the findings from a study conducted into the development of transferable skills at several educational institutions of higher education. Particular reference is made to establishing the value which students themselves place on embedded and bolt-on teaching approaches for developing their transferable skills.

Research

Several courses were investigated at the Education Department:

- Three from Institution 1 (embedded, integrated and bolt-on)
- Two from Institution 2 (integrated and bolt-on)
- Two from Institution 3 (integrated and bolt-on)
- Two from Institution 4 (embedded and bolt-on)

All four departments had previously collaborated on a project which considered the identification and dissemination of good practices for the enhancement of undergraduate transferable skills. Part of the outcomes from the project was the production of a handbook which could be used to support academics in developing transferable skills in their undergraduate students.

The Four Programs of Study

The departmental approach taken to enhance the quality of skills teaching is different for each of the four university departments involved in this study:

Institution 1: This department has been teaching transferable skills, incorporated into its curriculum for the past 5–8 years. About 80 percent of the student population undertakes a professional placement year. All three teaching approaches mentioned are used in this program. Examples of teaching techniques which accommodate the four mentioned approaches include student-led debates, students undertaking training for a peer tutoring role, and students undertaking practical problems not directly related to their discipline.

Institution 2: This department has a structured training program for the development of transferable skills, which has been running for about eight years and incorporates much in the way of integrated skills development. Examples of teaching techniques currently used include students assessing their peers' performance with respect to some specific activity within some predetermined assessment scheme and student teams from the same discipline undertaking a design activity.

Institution 3: many changes have been made to the curriculum in this department to include further skill development, which is currently embedded. The program now includes a couple of bolt-on skills development courses. Examples of teaching techniques used to accommodate the teaching approach include: external representatives working with small teams of students tutoring paper-based or practical problem-solving sessions.

Institution 4: transferable skills are mostly embedded and occasionally integrated into the curriculum in this department. Changes are currently being made to the curriculum so more skill-related activities can be included for the development of these skills. Examples of teaching techniques which accommodate the aforementioned approach include student teams undertaking a discipline-related, peer-assessed practical activity, and placing students in different teams for different tasks throughout a module.

Using Case Study Methodology

A case study methodology was used for this work, as it provided scope for an in-depth investigation to be conducted into the development of transferable skills in undergraduates. As such, it was possible to explore the particulars of the modules, especially in terms of gauging students' perceptions of the provisions in place to support their development of skills, as opposed to the generalities of a situation. It was possible to identify the relations of a number of variables and how they impacted upon student learning; identifying these links is considered an advantage of adopting a case study method. The subtleties of the four institutions could be investigated in addition to identifying key outcomes. A number of tools were used to collect data, including concept maps, focus groups, and questionnaires. The variety of tools helped corroborate findings through triangulation. Volunteer groups consisting of 5–7 students from each course were involved with this study and were asked questions about it to gauge their perceptions of their transferable-skills education. The students selected to form the research groups were representative of the peer group as a whole in terms of ability, gender, and ethnicity. As such, the majority of students were males who had gone straight into tertiary education.

The limitations of using a case study methodology were mainly that it was not possible to work with a large number of students when the objective was to gain an in-depth picture from a variety of rich data sources. The research was focused toward understanding student perceptions; therefore, the quality of the data would have been compromised if greater numbers of students had been used in the investigation.

Results

The results highlight questionnaire responses, which were readily quantifiable. Student responses were sought to the following two questions:

1. How do you feel you are learning/developing transferable skills on this course?
2. How do you judge the success of your development with respect to transferable skills?

In addition to which, a sample of comments from students attending courses in which both embedded and bolt-on approaches were used to teach have been shown. Although the numbers of students involved in the study may seem rather low, it should be appreciated that the selection of a case study methodology was useful for providing an in-depth study into skill development from what was assumed to be a representative group of students. Other data were also collected and analyzed as part of a wider investigation. Figures 1 and 2 illustrate samples of questionnaire data obtained from students attending courses taught using an embedded teaching approach to develop students' transferable skills.

Figure 1

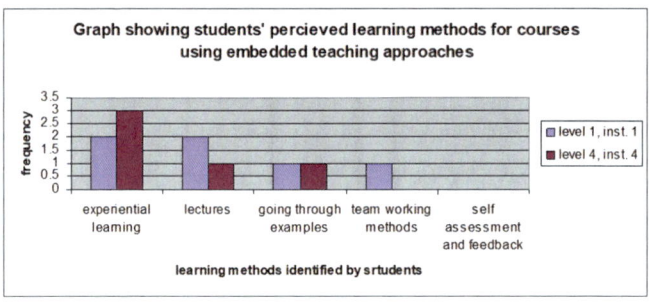

Figure 2

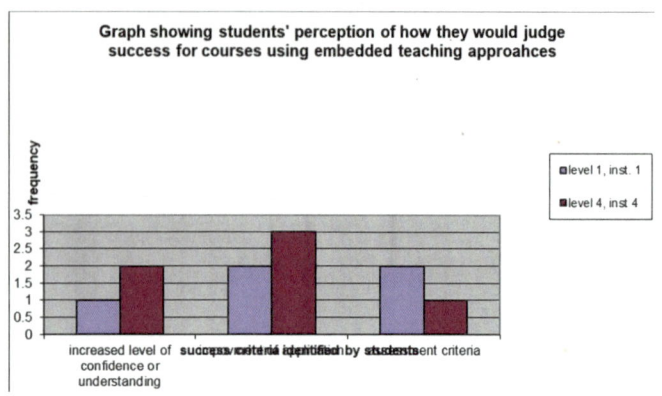

Sample comments of students' perceptions of their skill development were obtained from those attending courses in which embedded techniques were used to teach skills. These are shown below:

[We will learn] by being put into situations where we have to, so we're put into groups and told to carry out a task. To carry out a task, you have to work together, work as a team as well. I think that the lecturer is going to try and give us the responsibility of explaining things to other people.

Focus Group Response, Level 1, Inst. 1

- The course is a success, and then it should be easier to do the research project than if you had not done the course, but that's difficult to judge. You just know, it is when the design project finishes and you know whether it'll go well if you feel you could do it again.

Focus Group Response, Level 4, Inst. 4

- Figures 3 and 4 illustrate samples of questionnaire data obtained from students attending courses taught using a bolt-on teaching approach to develop students' transferable skills.

Figure 3

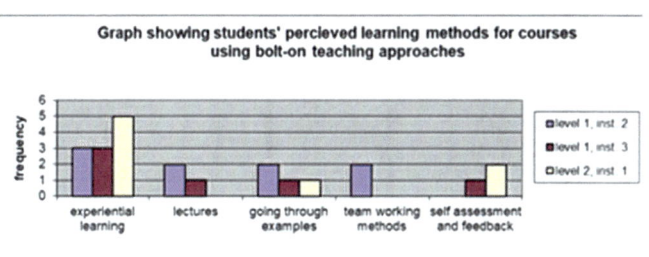

Figure 4

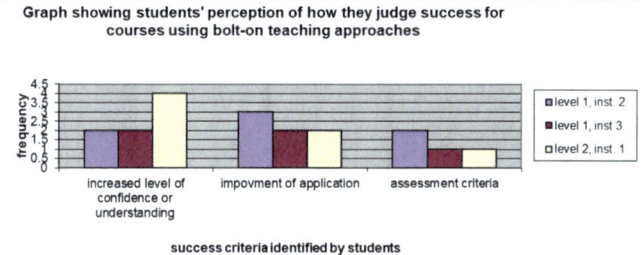

Sample comments of students' perceptions of their skill development were obtained from those attending courses in which bolt-on techniques were used to teach skills. These are shown below:

They'll probably also, because it's all about practice and being confident, and saying what you think in front of people. That's probably one of the key skills they'll try and teach us, and the only way to do that is just practice, practice, and practice.

Focus group response, level 1, inst. 2

But if you feel that there has been a change in your behavior and skills in a positive way after completing the module, then that can be counted as success.

Focus group response, level 1, inst. 3

It will make you more conscious about using skills and trying to communicate with people around you, especially people you don't get along with well and you don't know.

Generally, building confidence all around and getting us to do things.

Focus group response, level 2, inst. 1

Discussion of Results

The findings from the study suggest that the majority of students exposed to an embedded teaching approach for developing their transferable skills are aware of this 'implicit' development of skills. The majority of students feel that they are developing skills through experiential learning techniques. Students also seem to appreciate the value of developing skills in this manner, as the majority recognize an improvement in their application of skills as the deciding factor on which they would judge their success, even though they were not formally made aware of developing them.

The findings are in contrast to what is suggested in the literature, that more time could be spent explaining to the learner what skills are being taught and imply that students recognize a benefit to being taught skills which are embedded into the course or program. It is suggested that if, for example, group work is used by lecturers, opportunities are provided for students to explore their own ideas, problem solve, and discuss ideas with others. The learning is implicitly reinforced. Therefore, such a teaching approach should be routinely considered.

The findings also suggest that there is merit in bolt-on teaching techniques. There is probably little surprise in the perception of the majority of students that they develop their skills through experiential learning methods, but there is also some indication of 'learning through self-assessment or feedback'. The significance of this finding is to recognize this personal reflection as part of the learning process. Literature suggests that a capacity for self-assessment and the related notion of self-awareness are fundamental for maturing and progressing as a learner.

Being able to judge one's own performance is a valued attribute in both personal and professional contexts. It is also suggested that self and peer assessment give learners a greater ownership of the learning they are undertaking. As such, it could be argued that bolt-on teaching techniques provide opportunities for students to explicitly develop their abilities as self-assessors.

Another significant finding from investigating bolt-on teaching approaches is the importance students place on 'developing confidence' as a measure of their success. A recent survey conducted by the Higher Education Council

(HEC) suggested that recent graduates' employers place high relevance on their abilities to apply knowledge, analyze information, solve problems, etc. All of which are related to having the confidence to do so.

The findings from this study suggest that students recognize the relevance of learning skills through both embedded and bolt-on teaching approaches. Both approaches should be actively considered in addition to the more traditional integrated teaching approach to developing transferable skills within a higher education curriculum.

Further Research

To develop this work further, it would be interesting to consider whether transferable skills teaching is affected by the sequence in which teaching approaches are introduced to the curriculum. There is an implication, from having analyzed all the data, that the sequence in which various teaching approaches are introduced to the curriculum matters (students may reflect upon and relate their learning better at particular levels of study), but there is no evidence to justify this suggestion, which is worthy of further research.

Research suggests that nearly all transferable skills (and professional attributes) are required to a greater extent at work than they are developed during education. Further recommended research would be to investigate the transition from education to employment and whether the gap between the two is significant and how it could be narrowed. Having a consistent value of teaching is always important for a good education system. Therefore, curriculum can always be found in any education system. However, with different interpretations toward the term "curriculum," attitudes and values toward a pedagogical approach may vary, which in turn affects how students learn in schools. The term "curriculum" has different interpretations among scholars.

Rogers and Taylor (1998) define a curriculum as all the learning that is planned and guided by training or teaching organizations. In Arab countries, we are used to seeing curriculum in terms of the subjects that are taught through a series of books to cover educational objectives and allowing students to pass official exams with high grades. Thus, according to Tyler, curriculum evaluation is the process of matching initial expectations in the form of behavioral objectives with outcomes achieved by the learner. Taylor considers that all evaluations must be done in a way that takes into consideration the individual being assessed. In the age of technology, the aim of every school is to encourage skilled students and give them a good education, but how can a specific school attain this and how can we measure this success?

Curriculum typically refers to the knowledge and skills students are expected to learn, which include the learning standards and objectives they are expected to meet. Curriculum is more positive in nature, which could achieve the objective of motivating learning, enhancing knowledge and abilities, and developing positive values or even attitudes. It includes the units and lessons that teachers teach; the assignments and projects given to students; the books, materials, videos, presentations, and readings used in a course; and the tests, assessments, and other methods used to evaluate student learning. These elements could help achieve whole-person development of students. These two ideas are polarized, yet they are not contradicted with each other in the sense that they just view curriculum at either the macro or micro level. An individual teacher's curriculum, for example, would be the specific learning standards, lessons, assignments, and materials used to organize and teach a particular course. Every school should have a reliable curriculum with good learning objectives that are precise, measurable, and clearly stated. Today, with all the technologies and easy access to knowledge, the new objective should not only be to give knowledge and evaluate it but also to allow them to apply this knowledge in their real lives and widen their creativity. Educators have talked for years about curriculum development and curriculum design; some were concerned with the development of subject-centered curriculum, while others were concerned with implementing other kinds of curriculum that develop student critical thinking and allow for deep understanding, such as the integrated curriculum.

Lynn Stoddard, the author of 'Educating for Human Greatness,' describes the subject-centered curriculum as follows: "In this system, the main focus is on curriculum development (not human development), with subject specialists developing 'high standards' for student uniformity."

"—what our society believes all students should know and be able to do at grade-level check points. Teachers are told what and how to teach." He stated that "it is characterized by a common core curriculum, large classes, teachers treated as assembly-line workers, low morale, and much worthless testing." Leonard added that the aim of learning in this kind of curriculum is to merely pass the test, which is shallow and temporary, as he described. Today's student needs to develop thinking skills, content knowledge, social emotional competency, and critique thinking to face complex life and work competencies.

Chapter 3
Teacher Leader

Great Teacher Is a Great Leader

Teachers' Pledge

As a teacher, I pledge to teach my students with love and respect. I pledge never to ignore my students or label them.

I pledge to give them hope, motivate them, and let them believe in themselves.

I pledge to guide them down a road that is positive and life-giving. I pledge to be a good listener and trustworthy.

I pledge to grade their unique abilities and not let them feel obsessed with grades.

I pledge to be fair and honest and to use my power in the right way. I pledge to consider children's rights and give them to them.

I pledge to be a teacher leader.

A doctor's blunder may destroy a certain part of the body, while a teacher's blunder results in destroying the person who destroys society in return. The teacher's job is as important as a doctor's. Both have to create and/or influence a context for things to occur, which means creating understanding. A teacher has to create a context for learning, and a doctor has to create a context for healing. I truly believe that teaching is the most important job on earth, although not all deserve the title. Based on that, as much as the doctor work hard and be evaluated to be allowed to work in his field, a teacher should follow the same criteria and undergo a colloquium exam that decides if she/he deserves the title.

Teachers are in a sole position to have a direct impact on their students. Teachers can see their work in action, see the changes they affect, and, in so doing, they witness firsthand their goals coming to fruition. No matter what the goals are, we can sum them up in a single sentence: You want to help people. And there are many ways you can help someone as a teacher. To name a few, teachers aspire to educate, to inspire, to learn and to affect positive change.

Having the belief that every student can succeed and communicating that belief to students and parents greatly affects children's own belief in their ability to learn. Teachers should always remind them that she believes in them and expects them to work hard to be better than yesterday and not than anybody else.

A teacher who is eager to see her students doing well in their exams should keep in mind that amongst the students, a child will grow to be a creative artist, and he won't need to be proficient in math. There is an entrepreneur who won't practice history and literature in his/her career, and there is an athlete whose physical education is more important than physics. If the student doesn't get a great mark, continue to encourage him and help him build his self-confidence. Tell them they will not be judged by their scores and that mistakes are proof that they are trying. You are the catalyst of the school.

Being a good teacher is neither difficult nor simple. It all starts with the drive and perseverance to keep trying new approaches until the goal is accomplished. Everybody has a teacher or teachers they will never forget. Teachers are not only mentors, but also the manager, educator, and evaluator of their class, thus they must be sure that their work is not simple or undervalued. He or she is also a friend who listens to all students' difficulties and demonstrates empathy for them.

Teachers should love what they do! This love drives them to do their best, do what's best for students, and continually improve their practice. Their love for teaching makes it easy for them to share what they know. They not only share knowledge but also enthusiasm. They exhibit a level of enthusiasm that is infectious. Teachers and students around them notice this and are encouraged by it. You don't need a title or to have won an award, but you do need to be good at what you do to be taken seriously as a leader in your profession. Having a genuine belief that every student can succeed and communicating that belief to students and families greatly affects children's own belief in their ability to learn. When students believe they can succeed, they put greater effort into their learning.

A teacher should let students of all abilities know that she does not expect them to be perfect, but she believes in them and expects them to try hard. This gives them motivation to make the effort. Motivated students are willing to take on challenges and actually flourish in the face of problems. Highly quality teacher and student interactions are critical to student learning and development and an important part of best practice.

Each minute of the day is an opportunity to learn. Improving teacher-child interaction will assist students in meeting standards, lead to better academic outcomes for them, and build relationship that foster their social and emotional development. Learning is most effective when it relates to students' everyday lives and builds on what they already know. It is challenging but achievable, involves hands-on experience with concrete materials and is enjoyable, so that students want to pay attention and persevere with the task. Effective teachers avoid creating a negative climate, use of anger, harsh punishment, sarcasm, teasing, bullying, or humiliation. All of these make it more difficult for students to learn. Children who experience warm interactions and empathy have higher achievement.

Teachers should create a positive climate through many ways. For instance:

- Having a sense of humor and laughing at their own slip-ups; holding back-and-forth conversations with students; and encouraging students to respect and support each other and form positive relationships
- Showing enthusiasm for teaching and celebrating students' accomplishments
- Organizing and analyzing data in graphs and visuals is a way of teaching that permits students to ask

meaningful questions and dig deeper to solve problems. As a teacher, tolerating student to move beyond simply memorizing facts is a chance for them to acquire the skills of reasoning, inquiry, and communication.

- Stand in a systematized classroom and limit distractions: learning in a chaos place is not possible; there should be a healthy balance of structured and unstructured processes.
- Use music and voice inflection. It is a way that can recapture students' attention. A teacher can use a short song to finish up one task and move to another. Students might also respond well to varied voice inflection and tone, so use a mixture of loud, soft, and whispered sounds.
- Break down instructions into smaller, manageable tasks. It is best to use simple, concrete sentences. You might have to chunk the material you are giving to ensure your students understand it. You might even want to put the directions both in print and say them verbally. Be always careful not to give further instructions until a student has completed the previous task.
- Use multi-sensory strategies. As all children learn in different ways, it is important to make every lesson as multi-sensory as possible. Some students have difficulty in one area while they might excel in another. Get creative with your lesson plans, and students will appreciate the opportunity to use their imaginations or try something new; use a balance of structure and familiar lessons with original content.

"Responsibility Is the Price of Greatness."

"If you desire to lead, be the first one to put on your work gloves and dig in."

Winston Churchill

Teachers who are dedicated to their profession have similar qualities to leaders in other areas. They are not just thinking about themselves, but how their efforts will produce successes for all of those who are a part of their profession. They will experience many rewards—as long as you're not in it for the money.

Becoming a teacher leader is not difficult at all, but it requires a few simple performances:

- ***Be as excellent a teacher as you can be***. There's no need to try to change the world if you pay little attention to your own main responsibility of teaching.
- ***Identify problems, weaknesses, or opportunities.*** Teachers should push their students to succeed and not let them fail because the world is hard out there

and they should be able to face it. We say all children can learn, but actually, few of us really believe it. We locate the weakness and do not teach to strength. Every student can be a little better. Where do you see a need? Be willing to call it like it is and be a proactive part of a solution. Be a solution-oriented teacher.

- *Create concrete, realistic plans*: You may dream big, but you have to keep that in mind when you do your lesson plan, that is based on the resources found in school. The lesson plan should be realistic.

- *Be a professional, always which means be passionate about teaching and learning:* When unprofessional behaviors—like complaining, gossiping, taking shortcuts, missing responsibilities, and just producing poor work—sneak into your life, it discourages everything else you might be determined to do. As a leader, teachers should always be practicing their art and learning how to improve their techniques. They listen in class for opportunities to teach. One student's question can drive an entire lesson plan from which all students will benefit. Teachers look for explanations that present several concepts and perspectives to the students. These teachers watch their peers and learn from their teaching styles. They ask to be observed and for feedback on how to reach the students in their classroom. They are open to suggestions and to trying new things. They know how to quickly adjust their style.

- *Having commitment to the students and colleagues:* When one talks about a person's commitment to teaching, they are speaking of a deep connection with many people throughout the organization. They are dedicated to providing each student the best possible environment and tools for learning. They work with the parents to understand what challenges the students may have to learning and what approaches might work best with them individually.

- ***Embracing change and take risks***: As a teacher, you should keep in mind that every year you are going to meet new people and that class profiles can be different. The materials used in the classroom change. Administration and policies change. A great teacher knows this and anticipates change. They are daring to try new things and aren't hesitant to make modifications until they are as effective as they can be. It is important for teachers who consider themselves to be leaders to model a willingness to be early adopters of new ideas and innovative practices. Teachers should be risk-takers and willing to apply new methodologies even if they fail. Real leaders understand that not everything that they try will work, but they show resilience in the face of failure and never give up.

- ***Teacher leader should have self-efficacy and collective efficacy:*** When a group of teachers share the belief in their ability to positively affect students, it is commonly known as collective teacher efficacy. We should consider that the school is a pool, and each one throws his ideas where we can discuss to come out with the best idea. The work of teacher leaders must be to lift up their colleagues and build networks with them instead of competing with them. Many times, the most important work a teacher leader can do is to be a connector. If we can help connect our colleagues with materials, resources, and available support, we are doing our jobs well. The job of a teacher leader isn't to know more than their peers or to help build the capacity of their colleagues, but true teacher leaders should depend on their colleagues to build their capacity as well. Every teacher is a leader, whether they recognize it or not.

- ***Culturally responsive teaching is a pedagogy*** that knows the importance of including students' cultural references in all aspects of learning. A teacher leader should be aware of her/his own culture so that she/he understands how to interact with individuals from cultures that are different from theirs. This understanding helps them see their students and their families more clearly and silhouette policies and practices in ways that will help our students to succeed and this is what is called cultural competence. It is the key to thriving in culturally diverse classrooms and schools, and it can be learned, practiced, and established to better serve diverse students, their families, and their communities. Cultural competence is the ability to successfully teach students who come from a culture or cultures other than our own. It demands developing certain personal and interpersonal awareness and sensitivities, understanding certain bodies of cultural knowledge, and mastering a set of skills that, taken

together, underlie effective cross-cultural teaching and culturally responsive teaching.
- *Avoiding teacher burnouts*: Teaching is a rewarding yet demanding career. With long hours and a heavy load, it's easy to be a victim of teacher burnout. Without proper support, teachers are in danger of being overworked and not taking care of their own mental and physical health wellness. Psychology today describes burnout as "a state of chronic stress that leads to physical and emotional exhaustion, cynicism, detachment, and feelings of ineffectiveness and lack of accomplishment." Teachers and leaders are usually high achievers who like to work hard and are always looking for ways to improve. These traits are praiseworthy but can mean that educators fall prey to perfectionism and don't leave enough time for rest and recovery.

To avoid burnouts is accomplished by setting clear work boundaries. Perhaps that means you won't check your emails after 6 p.m., or you'll only grade papers until a favorite TV show starts, or maybe you'll never work on Sundays. To avoid burnout is to take time off. Make sure you have some time every weekend where school is the last thing on your mind. Each year, aim to take a vacation, even if you're staying at home. And take some of that much-deserved time off to catch up with friends or just hang out without thinking about school. As well as if you are sick, take the day off. Don't be a martyr—your students will be fine, so take care of yourself. As to the American Medical Association recently reported on the revival of doctors' lounges and how they can be used to combat burnout, Teachers, who also work in people-focused occupations, should look to build a sense of community and solidarity by using their teachers' lounges in a similar way. Time spent there can be a chance to refresh and re-join with colleagues.

The mind of a teacher leader is a growth mindset and not a fixed mindset.

The first difference between a teacher and a teacher's leader is that the teacher-leader has a growth mindset. They view things in different ways. They see mistakes as challenges. A teacher often possesses a staunch "My classroom, my students" mentality. This mentality focuses on how a teacher can best serve the students entrusted to them, and it implies a high degree of ownership over their classroom, curriculum, and student success. She sticks to what she knows and craves looking smart.

The teacher leader with a growth mindset, on the other hand, thinks, "Our students, our school." This mentality holds a bigger picture. Instead of strictly thinking about their individual classrooms, their focus is on the entire system that facilitates their teaching. While the teacher cares only about her class, a teacher leader cares about the whole school's growth.

This mentality inspires the teacher leader to do a few things that the ordinary teacher might not:

- First, they share. When something works well in their classroom, they are willing to help lead others to imitate that success; they are not selfish and greedy.
- Second, they team up with a team-oriented mindset. Teachers often feel like private contractors who do some "give and take" to get what they want. But a leader understands that when the success of the team surpasses the success of the individual every time.
- Third, they foresee it better. When the teacher leader looks at their school, they try to solve the problems instead of complaining, because complaining is the job of someone who doesn't want improvement. The teacher leader can see how improvements can be made and then takes truthful steps to achieve them.
- Fourth, they take on responsibilities beyond just their contractual obligations. The phrase "That's not my job" doesn't come from a teacher leader's lips often because she doesn't need a job description with the contract. Instead, if there's an opportunity to get behind a good cause in the school, they like to participate in that. Even without extra pay because they know that the school's success is one of her responsibilities and not only her class.
- Fifth, they accept the fact that they are not perfect and mistake is a challenge and not the end of the world, even if they shared their mistakes with their colleagues. They are in a continuous learning mode and trying to be better than yesterday and not than anybody else.
- Effective teacher learning is important for student achievement. Teacher learning is a continuous process that promotes teachers' teaching skills, helps them

master new knowledge, and helps them develop new proficiency, which in turn, help improve students' learning.

Research on that shows the importance of teacher's development and continuous learning.

Abstract

The aim of this research is to shed some light on the role of HR in achieving teaching efficiency, that involves acquiring relevant knowledge about students and using that knowledge to inform course design and classroom teaching. It also involves aligning the three major components of instruction: learning objectives, assessments, and instructional activities. HR target is to articulate explicit expectations regarding learning objectives and policies, prioritizing the knowledge and skills which we to focus on, recognizing and overcoming expert blind spots, and adopting appropriate teaching roles to support learning goals. And progressively refining courses based on reflection and feedback. This project is to know the various processes and activities that an HR can empower instructors by helping them develop a deep understanding of how students learn so that they can effectively apply and adapt teaching strategies to meet both goals and students' needs.

Introduction

1. Overview:

Human resource is a complex, multifaceted activity, often requiring us to juggle multiple tasks and goals simultaneously and flexibly. The powerful set of principles can help HR in maintaining both more effectiveness and efficiency in the choosing process of teachers by helping us creating the conditions that support student interest as well as teachers' benefit. Implementing these principles requires a commitment in time and effort, but it often saves time and energy later on.

2. Significance of the study:

The HR aim at the teaching and education level is to enhance theory, research, and practice through the publication of papers concerned with the analysis of teaching, teaching effectiveness, the factors that determine teachers' thought processes and performances, and the social policies that affect teachers in all aspects and stages of their careers. The journal will recognize that many disciplines—psychology, sociology, anthropology, economics, political science, history, and philosophy—have important contributions to make to the achievement of its goals, and the editors welcome contributions from them. In the absence of any dominant standard, the journal will allow a varied approaches to offer empirical research, theoretical and conceptual analyses, and reviews (both qualitative and quantitative syntheses) of high quality.

The purpose is to provide for student's education that will support their futures along with literacy, critical thinking, and creativity. Furthermore, the applicant who wants to get employed must be tested in a way to discover if they are cultured, wise, tolerant, and public-spirited to provide the ideal ways of educating as well as understanding students.

That's why HR aims to promote students' interest for developing a wise and knowledgeable person who can benefit by the techniques a school may provide him through information technology and education that may decide the future of economic development.

3. Problem statement:

In most schools' teachers are employed without obtaining effective training. The HR department's purpose is to find talent retention strategies, technical talent, a culture that suits the education system environment and communication skills with emotional intelligence, as well as demographic and technological changes which have been a major role in affecting the education system. The ways in developing and improving both the education sector as well as teacher benefits without considering the pace of time in training candidates efficiently, there are also include procedures to prevent student abuse mentally as well as consider teachers challenges with trying to expand and develop new concepts in education without excessive training, adding the generate of profitable ways and channel that change education in many wrong ways.

4. Questions:

- What are the best recruiting strategies that should be applied to hire the teachers and ensure placing the right person in the right place?
- What is the influence of training and development on teachers' performance?
- What measures should be used to evaluate teachers' performance?

5. Scope of the study:

- *Objective:*

HR helps empower instructors by developing a deep understanding of how students learn so that they can effectively apply and adapt teaching strategies to meet both goals and students' needs. For that we attempt, teachers should not be enrolled in teaching careers without passing the desired examinations that classify them according to their skills and knowledge of the education process and evaluate their performance through condensed development workshops, which help them sustain their current level of development and interact with the social, emotional, and intellectual climate of the course to impact learning. The HR department must consider all these equivalences. The importance of teachers is equivalent to doctors and engineers; they all hold a huge responsibility and should be trained and monitored to not commit mistakes. When an engineer did something wrong, he might kill people by the miss function of the building; when a doctor commits mistakes during a surgery, he might kill the patient; and when teachers mistake during the teaching process, they might abuse students and influence negatively on the society.

- *Purpose:*

The concentration of the HR managers is in identifying the best procedures for the education interest as well as the need to improve the traditional ways of teaching to more new ones. This can be done by recruiting candidates using the new techniques that can discover the hidden characteristics of each interviewed person with discovering how he/she can be a part of the improvement in the educational system adapted in schools.

Many can still be working on the old school policies that do not suit the development we reach now days. Today we have many technologies that can be used by tutors to make education a fun task. Also we can concentrate on the psychological side of each student, which can be considered a main part of his/her educational failure. That's why HR target is to recruit those who can achieve both efficiency and effectiveness in the educational sector.

6. Hypothesis:

H1: Teachers who pass through tests before hiring have better performances than teachers who get hired only after making a job interview.

H2: Schools that have an unqualified HR manager are less successful.

H3: The teacher evaluation program improves their performance, motivation, and discipline.

7. Methods and methodologies

Highlight the methods to both HR and educational challenges using values, ideal examples, conception reality ethical aspects, colloquium and scientific ideals.

The purpose is to understand and create knowledge information about how qualitative/quantitative methods will be done in order to achieve our target of proving that both the HR department and education department can together improve many things through several techniques.

- **Proposed solution methodology:**

Explaining through literature study, text interpretation, studies located on the Internet, and how they've been explored during the last few years.

Empirical studies will be conducted as Interviews with experts on the issues discussed in this project as an actual experience rather than theories or beliefs.

- **Methods:**

In this research we concentrated on how an HR department monitored and evaluated teachers' level of knowledge according to two indicators: effective teaching and learning rules, and we also used interviews with parents as well as teachers that helped in defining info about how of effective teaching was in every school. Also, from HR managers reported that how most teachers were actually learning effective teaching skills, and measured as indicators in the evaluation forms that were completed by students in the classroom.

- **Requirements:**

Teaching morals and ethics:

The terms ethics and values Education applies to all aspects of education that either explicitly or implicitly relate to ethical dimensions of life and are such that they can be structured, regulated, and monitored with appropriate educational methods and tools. A teacher's first moral obligation is to provide excellent instruction. Teachers with a high level of moral professionalism have a deep obligation to help students learn. Teachers with that sense of obligation demonstrate their moral professionalism by:

1. Coming to work regularly and on time.
2. Being well informed about their student-matter.
3. Planning and conducting classes with care.
4. Regularly reviewing and updating instructional practices;
5. Cooperating with, or if necessary, confronting, the parents of underachieving students;
6. Cooperating with colleagues and observing school policies so the whole institution works effectively.

- Understanding the foundations for moral and character foundation: Professionals in education need objective knowledge about how children form a basic sense of right and wrong and what schools can do to reinforce that appropriate development and provide that foundation. Research shows that children thrive on accomplishments, not on empty self-esteem messages. They do not become overburdened by reasonable pressures related to worthwhile activities, including demanding homework. The effects of positive and counter-productive child-rearing practices result in either positive or anti-social behaviors. Many of these practices are related to teaching.

Methodology

This section will be discussing about the method used in the research to analyze the need for a colloquium that concentrates on teachers who need to be evaluated as university doctors by an HR before being recruited. The aspects that we will be discussing include research design and data collection.

This study was descriptive research of the interviews done with many teachers who seemed to need more training in the domain they've been working in for years. There are many principles that have been interviewed by the researchers.

1. Research Design

To achieve the objective of the study, the research was conducted using a qualitative approach to obtain the necessary information. It is a multi-study by gathering of data to answer the research questions. The objective of quantitative research is to develop and employ mathematical methods, theories, and hypotheses pertaining to phenomena.

The research allows in-depth inquiry into the principals in the school perspectives on how they lead or manage the school in order to achieve the vision and mission of the school. This situation can lead to the conclusion that it is most appropriate to use a qualitative research design.

Usually in qualitative research, it is used widely in psychology, sociology, anthropology, and political science. Quantitative methods produce information only in the particular cases studied, and any more general conclusions are only hypotheses. Quantitative methods can be used to verify which of the hypotheses are true. Quantitative research can be considered as the most appropriate approach to studying educational issues that involve process as it aid in looking at the issues in depth.

2. Samples:

In order to get the information to answer the research question, the researchers choose interview method because it is a form of measurement that is very common in descriptive research. An interview is the most appropriate method to get as much information as possible in a single time. The data was collected through structured interviews with the eight principles, which were identified for the study, and through the reading of documents to study the way the school presented itself.

The interview for each principal took approximately around 30 minutes. Before carrying out the interview, an appointment was made beforehand with the principal. A set of questions was prepared that included background information of the principal, school background information, school management, school resources, and teacher appraisal in order to achieve school effectiveness. The principals also acknowledge to the respondents, all the information provided confidentially aspects of the interviews.

Results and Findings

This research is a study that concentrates on teachers without teaching experience in most of the Lebanon schools. It should be noted that the age group of 52.4% of teachers is 25–30 and the age group of 38.1% of teachers is 31–36. Where most of them graduated with majors' other than education.

Figure 1: The Age of Teachers in Lebanon

After conducting the interviews, the results were as following: 73% of teachers get employed after doing only a job interview. 19% of teachers pass through tests.

8% other

Figure 2: Selecting Strategy

Discussion and Analysis

The findings from recent research have tested the five features, with an emphasis on the results discussing several insights gained from this work and that have helped refine the framework. They are that:

- Changing procedural classroom behavior is easier than improving content knowledge or inquiry-oriented instruction techniques.
- Teachers vary in their response to the same professional development.
- Professional development is more successful when it is explicitly linked to classroom lessons.
- Professional development research and implementation must allow for urban contexts (student and teacher mobility).
- Leadership plays a key role in supporting and encouraging teachers to implement in the classroom the ideas and strategies they learned in their professional development.

1. Building ethical sensitivity and moral cognition

Courses in ethics with case problems and lectures on ethical theory do increase students' ability to reason through moral issues. The following examples of the impact of ethics courses on ethical sensitivity and cognition are drawn from engineering. Self and Ellison (1998) used Rest's Defining Issues Test (DIT) to assess if there was an increase in moral reasoning from students who took an ethics course. The researchers applied the test before and after the course and found a significant increase in reasoning capabilities.

Drake et al. (2005), using the DIT on assessing capabilities in moral reasoning, also found a significant increase between the beginning of a course and its end. The class size was 164 students, employing six teaching assistants. Such findings are widespread and well accepted—that discussions on moral practices and the teaching of ethical theory increase capabilities in moral reasoning.

The research, however, is almost 30 years old, with some of the original studies now almost eighty years old. We have not found recent studies that correlated courses on ethics with improved ethical behavior. The most we can be confident about is that courses do increase ethical sensitivity a strengthened ability to tell right from wrong. This ability in itself may lead to improved practices, but such improvements have not, for the most part, been verified.

2. *Extending the teaching of ethical practices*
a. Building the Course on the Ethical Issues

Two arguments can be developed:

- A new graduate without basic knowledge and experience will not be able to handle the pressure of different situations alone, which may lead to unethical practices.
- Ethical issues in discipline may be unclear; therefore, examining them in the classroom can help in clarifying what may arise in the profession as well as building skills that will help newcomers to be adequate and responsible when he/she enters a workplace. That is why a lecturer must suggest many situations that may happen along with providing training courses within the industry.

So, the ethical issues can be identified either from semi-structured, in-depth interviews or from early workshops.

b. Teaching Codes of Ethics

The belief that a code of ethics is sufficient to control ethical behavior is widely held.

- The results are determined primarily by interviews of users on the effectiveness of codes, and do tend to conclude that there is uncertainty about whether codes lead to more ethical behavior, so codes aim either to promote aspirations in terms of values or to control certain kinds of behavior.
- For strengthening codes, we need to document what has been developed by staff or members of the profession to identify and clarify their ethical problems, along with providing guidelines for possible responses.

Therefore, this leads us to ethics training programs that need to incorporate the development of a code which responds to the ethical issues faced by the organization or profession.

c. Public Interest Disclosures

In any organization, if your target is having an effective way to stop wrongdoing, we need to create an open culture with stress-free methods for exposing wrongdoing without the fear of losing their own job. That's why a disclosure (whistle blowing) is an effective way to ensure honesty and ethical behavior in which it's a motivator to make it an obligatory component of any course.

3. Teaching methods

This section examines pedagogical issues particular to the teaching of ethics. There are five that we believe warrant emphasis:

- Teacher skills and team teaching.
- Class sizes.
- Teaching across the curriculum
- The use of experiential learning techniques

The same concerns are relevant whether the ethics course is taught within an organization, be it public sector or private, or an industry association, or when taught at college or university classes.

Teacher Skills and Team Teaching

The question of whether a course should be taught by a specialist in ethics or a specialist in the discipline or profession is a long-standing one. We dismiss the arguments found in a number of journals that philosophy needs to be the dominant discipline. There are three necessary elements of any training course must be:

1. Workable codes of ethics
2. Managing public interest disclosures
3. Structuring an organization to handle its ethical issues

The primary teaching content of any ethics course must be the ethical issues faced by the discipline or organization.

This content demands that the basic skills of the ethics educator must be in the discipline itself, not in moral philosophy. We further argue that a low level of importance be given to teaching moral or ethical theories, and in fact, such theories that are needed are easily acquired by a discipline-based ethics teacher.

Class Sizes

We believe that ethics can only be taught in small classes. One argument behind small classes is that they encourage teacher/student or student/student interaction, where students learn from each other and from the lecturer. In these interactions, they come to understand their own ethical viewpoints and those of others more clearly. An increased ability to present to and convince others is an asset in persuading colleagues to adopt an ethical position. Such workplace skills can only be developed, in practice, in moderately small groups. Large undergraduate classes of 150 to 200 people are not conducive to this type of learning.

So, in our experience, for interactive presentations and discussions to work well, class sizes should not exceed about 30 people.

Teaching across the Curriculum

An issue that comes up in an academic environment is whether ethics should be taught as one separate subject or be incorporated into each of the principal units that comprise the academic qualification. Sims (2000) argues that it should be across the entire qualification, providing an example from his undergraduate business program. However, he also cites the arguments the other way—which ethics can be taught as a discrete unit. Business is multi-disciplinary, comprising several sub-disciplines (marketing, accounting, finance, human relations, strategic planning, etc.). In that context, the concept of incorporating ethical issues within the teaching of each sub-discipline is supportable.

The marketing lecturers would cover the ethical issues in marketing, the finance lecturers for their discipline, and so on. Even then, however, there needs to be a separate core common to all sub-disciplines. This core would include ethical theory, public interest disclosures, the underpinnings to a code of ethics (but not all content), and the common elements of the program intended to build personal and professional capabilities.

Experiential Learning Techniques

There is substantial support for the use of experience-based learning techniques in teaching ethics. The most common approach is the long-established case problem developed by the Harvard Business School. Nevertheless, there are other approaches. The advantage claimed is the further building of a trusting environment in which students can discuss personal viewpoints. This approach would also be of considerable benefit in workplace ethical training. Hemmasi and Graf (1992) argue that experiential exercises have several positive attributes: students retain material longer over time, are actively involved in the learning process, actual work environments are simulated, and students enjoy and engage more.

Case problems, as well as many other experiential techniques which are used in small groups, face the problem of the freeloader—students who do not prepare, leave the talking to others, etc. Litz (2003), however, offers some well-tried approaches for overcoming some of these problems.

4. Teaching and training guidelines
   i. Live Instruction.
   ii. Realistic case materials (over half the companies used case studies on ethics risks drawn from within their own organizations).
   iii. Comprehensive rollout (i.e., covering a large percentage of their employees).
   iv. Significant group interaction.
   v. Separate courses for compliance (coverage of the legislation that the company has to comply with).
   vi. Small class size.
   vii. Building decision skills rather than preaching
   viii. Use of a professional trainer.
   ix. Strong senior executive support.
   x. At least four hours of training.
   xi. New employee program
   xii. Follow-up, 2–6 months later.

Those of the 12 that can be applied to student classes reinforce the conclusions argued in this paper. Actual ethical cases drawn from the discipline and the building of decision skills on these cases rather than preaching, as well as group interaction and small classes, are common themes across the spectrum of training and teaching in ethics.

5. *Teaching standards*

Standards assist educators in evaluating accomplished teaching. The National Board for Professional Teaching Standards developed a process to determine whether a teacher possesses the attributes of accomplished teaching based on their standards in each of the certificate areas. In addition, many national organizations are working to develop standards to assist educators in improving curriculum, instruction, assessment, educator preparation, and professional development. The listed below provide resources related to standards development.

- Information Literacy Standards for Teacher Education
- Mathematics Teaching Standards
- The National Academy of Science's Teacher Preparation Standards
- The National Board for Professional Teaching Standards
- National Council of Accreditation of Teacher Education
- National Educational Technology Standards
- Science Teaching Standards
- Standards for Reading Professionals

Challenges

These new understandings and trends in teacher professional development are accompanied by several challenges. One major challenge to professional development in Lebanon is the tension between having multiple providers and trying to achieve coherence. As a result, the professional development teachers experience is often fragmented, with little continuity across professional development opportunities and little cumulative design. Professional development is offered under many auspices. Some professional development is offered by states, some by districts, some by colleges and universities, some by publishers, and some by independent consultants and organizations. Professional development has many different purposes. Some professional development is designed to support the implementation of a new curriculum or program; some to improve teachers' content knowledge in a discipline (e.g., algebra or biology); some is designed to support teachers in learning new approaches to pedagogy (e.g., differentiated instruction); and some is designed to focus on special populations (e.g., English language learners). Professional development is also funded and governed in many ways. And though the "one-shot" workshop has proven to be ineffective, some districts still use this model because they do not have the resources or capacity to design and provide more coherent, comprehensive professional development opportunities for teachers. Furthermore, it is difficult for schools and districts to obtain a comprehensive understanding of the professional development opportunities available or of any particular teacher's experiences (Wilson, Rozelle and Mikeska, 2011).

This multiplicity of professional development also makes it difficult to learn from studies of professional development. That is, professional development varies in so many ways that it is difficult to draw conclusions about which factors contribute to the success or failure of professional development efforts. Very specific features of professional development need to be manipulated to isolate their influence (see Penuel et al., 2011). Another challenge to studying professional development is that the tracking of teacher professional development is not strong in most districts. If districts did a better job of monitoring and recording the professional development experiences of teachers, these data could be used in longitudinal administrative data systems to help identify patterns of participation and eventually link those participation patterns with results for teachers and students. Another major challenge, as we discussed earlier, is being explicit about what teachers are supposed to learn from professional development. In many cases, the theory of action needs to be more completely specified than is typically done. For example, for a professional development designed to increase content knowledge, how is that knowledge expected to be translated into the classroom in ways that improve student learning? The explicit linking of ideas or behaviors taught in professional development to the text, lessons, and other material the teachers are using in the classroom has proven in many cases to be a powerful and perhaps necessary piece of the puzzle.

Conclusion

To help ensure that our vision for education is sustained. We believe that effective teacher training is key. In order for educators to bring about positive changes in education and successfully integrate technology to provide students with the 21st century skills they will need, they will need to be educated in new types of learning environments. In addition, professional development should be offered by school districts that are relevant and engaging. Teachers should also recognize all the professional development tools that can allow them to continue to learn about education while also evaluating and refining their teaching. Lastly, educators should become familiar with multiple ways to fund the changes and grants higher performance they want for their classroom that from testing themselves at "(EETT) Expert Education and Teaching Test" that will be considered as national standard for every teacher.

I truly appreciate this opportunity to share my research and knowledge, so I hope I have inspired many regarding the future of education.

I have identified and delved into some aspects of what I believe are the keys that will unlock the doors for public education through Curriculum and Pedagogy, Learning Spaces, and Sustaining the Vision. For that, I insist on "Teachers should not enter classes and education fields without passing the required tests, and WE ARE READY to ADVOCATE and EMPOWER for the KEYS TO SUCCESS!" My research presents more specifics on what our vision for the future of education is and how to sustain it.

Chapter 4
Assessment and Evaluation

"Many highly intelligent people are poor thinkers. Many people of average intelligence are skilled thinkers. The power of a car is separate from the way the car is driven."

– *Edward de BONO.*

Assessment is among an instructor's most essential educational tools. When properly developed and interpreted, assessments can help teachers better understand what their students are learning. The real goal of testing or assessment is to improve students learning. Students should study for the test in a way to understand the content and not memorize it. However, the scenario in our schools is different because the kind of examination is based on memorization and not understanding. Schools are competing to take the first rank. This ranking strategy is based on students' grades in official exams and standardized testing. That is the reason behind the increase in teaching to the test mentalities, which is destroying teacher, school, and student as well. All new titles state that there is a new step forward, which is 21st century skills focusing mostly on the four Cs, whereas 21st century skills are not new; they were known before. Socrates was talking about these 21st-century skills over 20 centuries ago. The Socratic Method is a form of cooperative argumentative dialogue between individuals that increases critical thinking. Teaching the child to take a good grade is another way of programming him to think that his intelligence is only a number on a piece of paper, killing his creativity and ignoring his talents. Education is not a curriculum to finish and a book to cover throughout a certain time to get a good grade at the end. It is the ability to be part of society and able to take decisions without depending on others. A good teacher does not follow the book. She/he uses the book to educate the child and prepare him for life, as EINSTIEN once said, "Education is what remains after you get out from the school."

On the other hand, teachers as evaluators should use different kinds of assessment to evaluate children, provide appropriate feedback on students' performance, record students' results to motivate them to work harder and to improve their work before theirs, and even change methods of teaching. Students should be able to evaluate themselves.

"I am calling on our nation's governors and state education chiefs to develop standards and assessments that don't simply measure whether students can fill in a bubble on a test but whether they possess 21stcentury skills like problem solving and critical thinking, entrepreneurship, and creativity."

President Barack Obama, March 2009.

From no child left behind to a better way of teaching, we do not only want to put all children in schools but we also have to know what to teach and how to assess. A good assessment is valid, fair, and ethical. As President Obama has noted, much more than "bubbling in" on a test. Students need to be able to discover, estimate, produce, and use knowledge to solve problems.

It also needs students to attain well-built thinking, problem solving, plan, and communication. Assessment and evaluation are probably the most difficult, if not the most controversial, challenges teachers' face. There are no easy answers, nor is there a program to follow—the business of assessment is based on different transactional teaching and learning.

The standardized test is not fair and behind the turnout of children. In my experience, we program our children to work for the test and not to learn; we are destroying them under the name of testing them. Many students have exam phobias because of tests.

In education, the term assessment refers to the wide variety of methods or tools that educators use to evaluate, measure, and document the academic readiness, learning progress, skill acquisition, or educational needs of students. Personally speaking as to what is going on in the official exam is a tragedy. Success is achieved by studying a book that has exams from previous years; there is a great probability of having the same questions. From this point, you can see how unfair and invalid they are and to what degree they are objective. Most of the standardized testing is studied through using a sample book of questions as a criteria student follow to succeed. We are simply testing our children to the test. We are killing creativity; children can be part of those who produce the test not consume it.

Tests by themselves cannot improve educational outcomes unless they are prepared in a way that promotes learning. There are different ways of evaluating a child and assessing him/her.

While assessments are often equated with traditional tests—especially the standardized tests developed by testing companies and administered to large populations of students—educators use a diverse collection of assessment tools and methods to measure everything from a four-year-old's readiness for kindergarten to a twelfth-grade student's comprehension of advanced physics. Just as academic lessons have different functions, assessments are typically designed to measure specific elements of learning—e.g., the level of knowledge a student already has about the concept or skill the teacher is planning to teach or the ability to comprehend and analyze different types of texts and readings. Assessments should also be used to identify individual student's weaknesses and strengths so that educators can provide specialized academic support, educational programming, or social services and not just give them a grade. Assessment should be developed in a way that shows students weaknesses or misunderstandings in order to re-explain what is not understood and to give a grade. Assessments should be used for a wide variety of purposes in schools and education systems, and there are qualitative and quantitative assessments.

PISA has emphasized that tests should evaluate the student's deeper conceptual understanding, which is the ability to use their knowledge and not only memorize the content. As educationalists, we cannot deny that traditional assessment methods and standardized testing do not properly evaluate the skills needed to prepare learners for working in the modern world. Skills such as critical thinking and problem solving, communication, collaboration, creativity, and innovation are all vital traits for students but are not currently measured effectively by most countries.

Schools should prepare their students with the skills that they need to work in the new market and with new mentalities that can face the challenges they will be facing in this century. Thus, educators need to build a new kind of assessment strategies other than standardized testing, which is like a one-way ticket.

"Everybody is a genius, but if you judge a fish by its ability to climb a tree, it will spend its whole life believing that it is stupid."

Albert Einstein

Testing intelligence through a standardized test that is considered to fit all is a reason behind losing brainy people. Teachers have always used a recall test, or by asking questions, that shows to what extremity the content was memorized. Many successful people dropped out of school and turned out to be very intelligent. Many students have been traumatized by experiencing extremely stressful moments. Others are having exam phobias because the test for them is understood as a one-way ticket other than the reaction of parents when the students fail.

In fact, integrating 21st-century teaching practices should start with updating teachers' assessment strategies. There is a need to make strategies and tactics in schools that encourage students to become critical and creative thinkers, problem solvers and so that they collaborate and communicate effectively. Brian Wibby in his article stated that the National Education Association, in partnership with education leaders and several other national organizations considered the four Cs (critical thinking, collaboration, communication and creativity) as the key factors in preparing young people to compete and collaborate with others in our globally interconnected world (Webby, 2016). That was too what Saxena considered "Consistent and consolidated focus on these 21st-century skills transform students from being disempowered in their education and not understanding its purpose or relevance by being asked to do things with their knowledge and care about it and to use it purposefully." (Saxena, 2013). In other words, the teachers' practices should not be instructing and spoon feeding the content but allowing understanding. Students need to be provided with such educational experiences to be able to move to a new globalization 3.0 era (Friedman, 2007). The PISA findings show that there is a positive association between students' performance and their approaches to learning, such as their motivation to learn, their emotional intelligence and their learning strategies. These learning approaches are not only associated with success in exams but are also considered an educational outcome on its own: once students leave school, they must be able to establish goals, to persevere, to monitor their learning process, and to adjust in the real world. Finally, despite the fact that there exists a variance in the degree those sets of skills were taught in schools, it seems teachers are not fully prepared to address and asses these skills. As to a research I have made, it seems that teachers' perceptions outweighed their personal description of practices. They were positive about themselves addressing critical thinking skills, collaboration skills, communication skills, creativity and innovation skills, and self-direction skills. However, they did not claim to be assessing such skills. Teachers' practices were a way far from being at the level of 21st-century schools as described by Partnership for the 21st century (P21, 2011). In other words, students of the 21st century are still being taught with methods of previous century. In terms of teacher practices findings showed that, teachers stated that the majority of students use technology for self-learning one to three times per month, which is, too low but most of them do not select the appropriate technology such as Glogester, Edmodo, Docs teach, Chigger, Kahoot, Quizlet... On the other hand, the results indicate that there is low usage of technology by the students to analyze information and the majority of the teachers did not really assess students' skills in using technology for learning. Thus, through their own lenses, teachers considered themselves not addressing technology skills and they did not assess those skills, as it was not part of the grading system.

Schools are still not doing a great job of assessing these important skills that students need to succeed in the 21st century for college work and citizenship. In the absence of a system that examines those sets of skills, it is difficult to judge if the system is indeed addressing them. According to Wagner (2008), 21st century education needs to start with assessment, and what you test is what you get. So, by declaring that they did not assess such skills at all or poorly, teachers are assuring that 21st-century skills remain lagging behind in schools. Results of my study show that despite knowing these skills, teachers were too far from addressing and assessing these skills, which is similar to previous studies that found out teachers' practices were way far from being at the level of 21st century schools as described by Partnership for the 21st Century (P21, 2011). Finally, sadly, that is easier visualized than realized, with myself included. Too often, I teach, and then I test what I taught. This process is far too common in all grade levels, primarily due to the lack of time and energy to plan. Unfortunately, this traditional method does not help the teacher or the students to maintain a laser-like focus on what really needs to be learned. The testing-after-the-fact mentality promotes mind-dump learning. A more accurate means of measuring students' progress toward mastery of communication, collaboration, critical thinking, and creativity (4C) skills would be to measure those skills directly in students. This needs the development of a tool, united to the Partnership for 21st Century Learning framework of 21st century ready skills that could measure student proficiency in each of the 4C areas (Partnership for 21st Century Skills, 2007). My study highlights the problem of students lacking the four C skills as they enter the workforce. This problem is critical in our digital age because it reveals a gap in our education system's ability to adequately prepare students to succeed in college, in a career, or as responsible citizens capable of making good decisions in a global economy. Whereas ignoring this problem prevents the country to be competitive in the world marketplace. Furthermore, the problem cannot be solved if our aim is to succeed the official exam because it is the only entrance we must pass through to continue our education. We are simply teaching to the tests, where the tests are only repeated even in the universities, and as to my experience, a student can pass the exams only if he has prepared and solved the old ones.

My study also showed a significant difference between how to assess using the four Cs rubrics and the way students are assessed through standardized exams. It shows weak to never assess these skills or use any of the rubrics.

The aim of educating a child is to help him succeed in life. In this century, many changes occurred that recommended a change in the educational system. The "21st Century Skills" movement is more than a decade old. In 2002, the Partnership for 21st Century Skills (P21) with the assistance of the NEA began a two-year journey to develop what became known as a "Framework for 21st Century Learning," stating 18 different skills. In the last eight years, 16 states have joined P21 and agreed to build 21st-century outcomes into their standards, professional development, and assessments. After several years of research (P21, 2010), it was concluded that the framework of 21st century skills is too long and complicated. To solve this issue, four specific skills were considered the most important and became known as the "Four Cs" which includes critical thinking, communication, collaboration, and creativity. Being in a complex, demanding, and competitive century, students are obliged to learn more than the 3R's (Reading, Writing, Arithmetic) they are tested on in school. It is time to help them go above and beyond by the implementation of the 4Cs in our curricula—communication, collaboration, critical thinking, and creativity (P21, 2002). Many researches have been done related to this topic. Consequently, for the past 10 years or so, there has been a growing appreciation for the importance of skills other than the cognitive skills typically tested by standardized tests.

In 2008, British secondary school curricula were reconstructed to emphasize these skills, and pilot programs have begun measuring these skills. The European Union designated 2009 as the European Year of Creativity and Innovation, and they began holding conferences and funding relevant teacher trainings and problem-based learning curricula. Moreover, China has begun massive education reform in order to replace its traditionally rote teaching style with a more problem-based learning approach. Japan as well has begun to implement educational and economic improvements to address its creative skills' issues. The four Cs represent the way we utilize the acquired knowledge. It is a major key for teaching students a deep understanding of knowledge and simplifying the transfer of that knowledge to new environments. Schooling in this century is providing students with these skill sets in order to prepare a generation capable of facing the real world successfully (Milestones for Improving Learning and Education [MILE], 2002). Researchers argued that these skills should be both part of the school curriculum and integral to the academic content. Herrington and Kervin (2007) argued, "A thinking curriculum is one that provides a deep understanding of the subject and the ability to apply that understanding to the complex, real-world problems that the student will face as an adult." (p. 64). Educators should engage students and allow them to be critical thinkers, collaborators, communicators, and creative people (Pearson, 2017). Creativity can be defined in many ways, but P21 defines creativity as the use of new ways of idea creation technique. It is to understand and use knowledge to get with new ones. Robert Sternberg of Tufts University said, "People are not born creative or uncreative, they develop a set of attitudes toward life that characterize those who are willing to go their own way. Some attitudes toward life are the willingness to (a) solve problems in novel ways, (b) take risks, (c) "sell" ideas that are new and out of the box, (d) persist in the face of obstacles, and (e) observe if their own preconceptions are interfering with their creative process." (Sternberg and Lubart, 1991). Actually, without imagination and investigation of ideas, our collective fund of knowledge would languish. We do need assessments to determine what students learn and understand, but we can integrate imagination in the creation of those assessments to ensure that students' creative thoughts and higher executive functions are incorporated into their assessment experiences. Creativity should be encouraged along with practical knowledge since it is multidisciplinary, allows self-discovery, promotes thinking and problem solving, and allows a student to enter his happy zone and have fun.

On the other hand, from solving problems in class assignments to facing world situations, critical thinking is a valuable skill for students to master. Critical thinking is the ability to analyze and evaluate the way you think (Morgan, 2002). However, the current vision of schools is to standardize curriculum and concentrate on test scores. This approach to teaching will weaken educators' ability to address critical thinking in the classroom because it stresses on "teaching to the test" (Wong, 2007). The four-century skills are important for both students and educators. "If elements of the 4Cs are integrated into student learning, then we can help raise them a greater sense of community for 'Collaboration' and boost them to work together to embark upon 'Critical thinking' and be involved in problem solving." (Saxena,

2013). In an attempt to respond to the challenges of 21st century skills, the Partnership for 21st Century Skills (P21) was established in 2002. The purpose of P21 is to investigate the skills needed by students to reserve a spot for themselves in the global economy (P21, 2011). In this line, the partnership highlighted: (1) critical thinking; (2) communication; (3) collaboration; and (4) creativity as essential skills for the 21st-century knowledge economy. These have been termed as the four Cs of the 21st century learning and were considered to be bolstered by other skills, on top of which were technology skills, life and career skills.

How to Implement the Four Cs

To achieve a 4C's-aligned classroom is through new teaching methodologies. "There is not only one tool to rule them all in education. Any tool that is worthy of consideration by a teacher, it should first clarify how it will affect student learning." (Pace, 2015). "Teachers should be supported in making them happen in the classroom for each student to embrace the four Cs (critical thinking, communication, collaboration, and creativity) and embed them through professional development for the teachers, in the curriculum, and in assessment. (Kay, 2011) A new learning menu must be flexible and adaptable includes blended learning, flipped classroom, gamification, and other ways to engage the students. Because of technological and pedagogical developments, one of the popular active learning approaches today is the flipped classroom. The flipped classroom approaches are made up of two strategies in and out of the classroom (McLaughlin, 2016). As to this approach, student prepares the lesson through googling and then come to class, which is a transformed strategy of the traditional teaching that increase self-directed learning." Flipped classroom is to improve student learning and achievement by reversing the traditional model of a classroom and focusing class time on student understanding rather than on lectures. To accomplish this, teachers post short video lectures online for students to view at home prior to the next class session. This strategy can help the teacher to use the class time in mastering the material through collaborative learning exercises, projects, and discussions. (ACEDO, 2005) This approach forces a student to understand the topic before coming to class which allows permanency of knowledge. (Dawson, 2015). On the other hand, "Gamification" Games as Albert Einstein stated are the most elevated form of examination. He considered games are avenues for something deeper and more meaningful than a childish waste of time. "These are created for the players to crack an obstacle and permits communication, cooperation, and even competition among the players. Most of the games are designed with rich narratives that helps in building creativity and imagination amongst their players (Schaaf and Quinn, 2017). It is the use of game mechanics to increase student's commitments to the learning environment as well as to motivate and to encourage learning by thinking in harmony with game logic (Kapp, 2012). Moreover, several learning methods are tackled in the blended learning training (Kaplanais, 2013). For the past decade, many researchers have stressed the importance of a shift in teachers' practices implementing the four CS. Nevertheless, there has been very little focus on the professional development of the teacher. The framework emphasizes the importance of flexible and adaptive learning contexts that allow for both formal and informal learning inspire by a sense of community. On the other hand, the framework suggests that teacher professional development programs need to be:

- Observed and teachers are involved in concrete tasks of curriculum design, implementation, and assessment;
- Learner-centered: grounded in teachers' own questions, problems, and issues
- Collaborative: built based on the collective experience of participants and the wider community
- Relevant and applicable: related to teachers' work and contexts
- Continuous and on-going support during and after the program.
- Integrated with other aspects of school reform.

Assessing the 21st Century Skills

Student assessment, whether by standardized tests or class-room-based measures, is a cornerstone of effective teaching and learning (P21, 2007). In fact, assessment is the driving force behind quality instructional practice, and it stands to reason that if assessment can be upgraded to address 21st century skills, then instructional practices will follow (Wagner, 2008: p. 17). With the passage of the No Child Left Behind Act of 2001, testing has become routine and focused on important content fields. The results of standardized testing are used to determine whether students can move on to the next grade and to judge the quality of schools and the educators who work in them. Recently, educators and policymakers have been examining and studying to what extent the current assessment tools measure the skills needed to succeed in the 21st century workplace and not only knowledge. The Partnership for 21st Century Skills believes that there is a need for a shift in our assessment tools. "We must move from largely measuring discrete knowledge to measuring students' ability to think critically, examine problems, gather information, and make informed, reasoned decisions while using technology." (P21, 2007). According to Wagner (2008), the assessment system is the starting point for any school that decides to teach the 21st century skills. However, the importance of assessment for learning has gone largely unexploited because we have failed to deliver the proper tools into the hands of teachers and school leaders (Association for Supervision and Curriculum Development [ASCD], 2011). If we are to fulfill our mission, we must evaluate the quality of our assessments at all levels and in all contexts. Traditionally, we consider scores are a valid and reliable inference about student's achievements. However, we must recognize that assessment is more than the test score's dependability—it also has to be about the score's effect on the learner. Even the most valid and reliable assessment cannot be regarded as high quality if it causes a student to give up. We must begin to evaluate our assessments in terms of both their quality and their effect on future learning. Above all that with the knowledge expansion and the global economy, schools are obliged to prepare their students with the skills that they need to work in the new market and with the new skills that are required to face the challenges (Shall, 2016). As students become more aware of the importance of what they are learning, they become more motivated. Thus, educators need to build assessments for learning rather than assessments of learning. (Stiggins and Chappuis, 2006). Based on the aforementioned, when investigating whether a school addresses four C skills or not, it is essential to investigate their assessment procedures. In the absence of a system that examines those sets of skills, it is difficult to judge if the system is really addressing them.

How Can We Assess the Four Cs?

We lose too many talented people by defining intelligence through exams that are narrowing and standardized. Teachers have always used recall tests or by asking questions that show to what extent the content was memorized, but researchers are beginning to understand that assessment can play an important role in supporting learning. Moreover, some did not believe in standardized testing and considered many successful people to have dropped out of school and turned out to be very intelligent. A grade should not be a standard way to evaluate intelligence. In fact, integrating 21st century teaching practices should start with updating teachers' assessment strategies that they use in the classroom to support their teaching rather than only using standardized testing. Education experts recommend a balanced approach to using formative and summative assessments and believe that both types are important to improve teaching and learning. Assessment must be used as an instructional tool for use while learning is occurring (formative), and as a tool to determine if learning has occurred (summative). (Partnership for 21st-century Skills, 2007). Researchers describe six assessment tools and strategies that impact teaching and learning as well as help teachers raise a 21-century learning environment in their classrooms:

(Rubrics, 2) Performance Based Assessments (PBAs), 3) Portfolios, 4) Student self-assessment 5) Peer assessment, 6) Student Response Systems (SRS).

1. Four C Rubrics:

Is an assessment strategy that measures students' knowledge and ability. A rubric permits teachers to measure certain skills that cannot be measured by standardized testing (Reeves and Stanford, 2009).

For example, the presentation rubric for PBL includes criteria that we can use to grade a student's creativity and critical thinking in his project, whereas the content should be assessed separately.

2. Performance based assessments (PBA):

PBA are used to evaluate students' knowledge about a topic and their ability to apply what they know in a real-world situation. PBA includes designing and constructing a model; developing, conducting, and reporting on a survey; carrying out a science experiment; writing a letter to the editor of a newspaper; creating and testing a computer program; and outlining, researching, and writing an in-depth report (Darling-Hammond and Pecheone, 2009). Wiggins and McTighe stated, "Performance assessments are a way to teach not only how to assess but also what kinds of performance challenges are actually considered most important in a field or profession." (2005).

3. Peer assessment

Peer assessment strategies can improve the quality of learning, and the test will be another way of teaching if done correctly in the correct way (Topping, 2009). Students do peer assessment themselves, where older students may assess younger students or a high achiever can assess a low achiever. Topping (2009) considers that peer assessment works best when students are asked to provide formative and qualitative feedback rather than simply grading or giving a score to peers.

4. Students self-assessment

It is a formative assessment, whereas a student evaluates himself.

Teachers permit their students to take a leading role in their own education. Teachers who allow students to be little teachers are engaging them in the process of thinking about and assessing their own work so they can better understand their mistakes and take responsibility of it. It is a way to build their character (Dyer, 2015). This can take the form of "I can" statements, learner contracts, reflections, portfolio reviews, and recording oneself. Researchers considered that the most effective rubric is one that involves students in the formation of the evaluation process that raises meta-cognition, encourages active participation, and eventually puts students at the center of the learning process (McMillan and Hearn, 2008). Moreover, he will not only think deeper but also create a sense of responsibility and develop critical thinking skills (Andrade and Valtcheva, 2009).

5. Portfolio assessment

Portfolios are students work gathered over time and used as a summative evaluation method. It shows student effort, development, and achievement for a period; than being a snapshot of a student's knowledge at one point in time (like a single standardized test). It measures a student's ability to apply knowledge rather than simply memorize it. They are considered both student-centered and reliable assessments of learning (Anderson, 1998). Portfolios are one of the most flexible forms of assessment, as they are used across subject areas and grade level to report student progress, compare achievement across classrooms or schools, and to increase parent involvement in student learning.

6. Student response system

Is to use many kinds of technology-based formative assessment tools that can be used to measure students' abilities and understanding of the material. Through the integration of hardware (hand-held clickers, receiver, PC, Internet connection, projector and screen) and software, teachers can ask students a wide range of questions (both closed and open-ended), where students respond on the spot, and the teacher then displays the data immediately and graphically. The usefulness of such an assessment is that the teacher can directly examine students understanding and then finding new teaching strategies to maximize it. (Beatty and Gerace, 2009). This kind of assessment allows the teacher to collect and display data immediately rather than waiting days to present the outcomes, as with a test, essay, or project.

According to researchers SRS, when integrated effectively into instruction can:

- Improve engagement
- Increase critical thinking
- Give students a voice in classroom decisions
- Improve classroom discussion
- Increase attendance and retention, and finally
- Increase enjoyment of class (Beatty and Gerace, 2009).

Conclusion

The aim of educators is to help their students succeed in life where technology is prevalent in every aspect of their lives. Hence, digital literacy requires teachers to make the shift from passive technology usage to thoughtful applications of technology to create new content and process information at higher levels through infusing the four Cs into all applications of technology in the classroom. The Partnership for 21st Century Skills believes that such a shift to the widespread adoption of four Cs in our schools pushes us to move from measuring the content to measuring students understanding of the content and their students' ability to think critically, examine problems, gather information, and make informed, reasoned decisions while using technology. Similarly, the 21st-century skill assessment should focus more on a student's operational skills and preparing them to face challenges of tomorrow and getting fit in the digital world. Two other aspects of the framework include the learning environment and the professional development for teachers conducive for the realization of the framework (P21, 2011).

Teachers agree that there's too much testing in schools, but well-designed classroom tests and quizzes can improve student recall and retention. Instead of standardized tests, students should have tests created by teachers with the goal of learning more about the students' abilities and interests. The image of students sitting in silence filling out bubbles, computing mathematical equations, or writing timed essays causes a negative reaction. But educators shouldn't give up on traditional classroom tests so quickly but they should design and administer them with format, timing, and content in mind—and a clear purpose to improve student learning. The role of teachers is very important, the teachers work as facilitators, whose role is to aid the student and not giving a lecture, but to guide by the side. Moreover, teachers must challenge the student by making them effective critical thinkers and not being merely a 'teacher' but also a mentor, a consultant, and a coach. In today's classrooms, teachers have to construct a lesson that allows students to "make meaning through mindful manipulation of input" (Fogarty, 1999, p. 78). Sawyer suggests that the role of the teacher has shifted from being considered the "sage on the stage," to the "guide on the side" (Sawyer, 2006, p.4), facilitating learning for students. Instead of being regarded as the "font of all wisdom" (Ryland, 2011), they are an active member of the classroom whose focus is to ensure that all the students are learning. Such a shift of role allows students to contribute to the classroom understanding of a concept and have opportunities to learn from everything, including classmates, exams, technology, projects, etc., not just the teacher. Thus, administrators need to support teachers with effective professional development and the needed resources to achieve the plan. When our students have the cognitive foundation to learn how to learn, they can discover what else is "out there" in our world. On the other hand, the process of learning does not shut down during assessment. Parents are more concerned about test scores rather than student self-concepts and learning strategies. Assessments are tailored to specific modules and teaching situations. Assessment is not an ending activity, but rather an ongoing process that helps the student continue to learn. Similarly, students of our digital age should acquire the 21st-century skills that will pave the way for them to excel in today's job market. Students now must be able to show that they can be collaborators, communicators, creators, and critical thinkers.

Chapter 5
Assignments

Parents, on the other hand, have to step up and emphasize education, do assignments with their kids, and be proactive in enhancing children's education. As parents, you can't just drop your kid off at school and assume he'll end up at Harvard. No kid can study effectively if they don't have enough to eat, if their parents are on drugs, if the home environment is chaotic, or if the parents are not involved. Parental involvement is very important in achieving the learning process. Homework is an opportunity for the children to practice skills learned at school as well as minimize stress and maximize learning for the children. As a teacher, I was always thankful to each and every mom who helped me with her kids, and we even collaborated to prepare a lesson plan. They were the secret soldiers behind their sons and daughters' success.

Dealing with homework is a big stress for students and teachers. Homework should not be like a medicine with an ugly taste; we can add strawberry flavor through using new tactics. Teachers should be aware of these points when giving homework.

- Does it boost our students' homework completion rate with these highly motivating materials?
- Does this homework ask each student to practice something that the student has not yet mastered?
- Does the student clearly know the benefit from it?
- When students are asked to do any task, is it copied or done with carelessness?
- What other teachers gave as homework?
- What is ethical and achievable?

Homework should not be a burden. It should be a positive experience that encourages children to learn. Teachers assign homework to help students review, apply, and extend students investigation of a topic more fully than class time permits.

Many researchers conducted a lot of studies to show the relation between homework and academic achievement. With only rare exceptions, the relationship between the amount of homework students do and their achievement outcomes was found to be positive and statistically significant.

Cheating Is the First Step Toward Building a Criminal Mind

There are probably as many ways to cheat as there are students, but some basic types crop up again and again—even if the methods change over time, from peering over a classmate's shoulder to texting an answer under the desk.

- Copying another student's answers or homework
- Letting another student copy your answers or work

- Using or distributing copies of test questions, answers, or answer keys.
- Secretly using "crib notes" or the Internet to help you answer test questions, whether you've printed a cheat sheet on your leg or looked up information on your phone.
- Having someone else do your homework or take a test for you, or doing the same for another student.
- Changing your answers on a test after it's been graded and then asking for the grade to be changed.

We all think of a suitable punishment for cheating, but did we ever think about the reasons behind cheating—what makes him cheat and why?

"I'm a dedicated student, but when my social studies teacher bombards me with 30 questions due tomorrow or when a teacher gives me a report and worksheets on a night when I have swim practice, praying, gym, and other homework—I'm going to copy from a friend!" One of my students told me when I asked him, "Why are you cheating?" Similarly, some of my students considered that their assignments are pointless. Some students are not motivated by what they are taught, so they copy the assignments so they do not waste their time on something of no interest to them.

Students who use cheating as a way to success are building a criminal mind in an indirect way. It may seem so simple and normal, but it is not always true. Cheating is a dishonest behavior that alters a person's sense of right and wrong, so after cheating once, some students stop viewing the behavior as immoral. Many factors, such as stress, interruptions, and a lack of study skills, lead to cheating in academic settings. One of the main factors that cause students to cheat is the pressure and stress rotating accompanied with exams and grades. Cheating in school associates with cheating later; it carries over to other activities. It correlates with cheating in one's professional life and with other misbehaviors.

Homework shouldn't be a nightmare or a punishment. Both the quantity and quality of homework are to be considered when giving homework. As well as training seminars should be given to how we give homework because when we design homework, we design a lesson plan. It is an art of teaching.

Homework improves your child thinking and memory, encourages him to use his time wisely, and allows him to review what has been covered in class. You can help your student avoid the temptation to cheat at school. Take care to put just the right amount of scholastic pressure on the child. Too little and he gets lazy and bored and becomes unfulfilled and unhappy; too much and he either gives up or cheats to achieve. Try to find the balance that fits your student. Homework is best appreciated when it helps your children use resources such as libraries, reference materials, and computer websites to find information. It allows him to extend his learning by applying skills to new situations.

As a teacher, these are some pieces of advice that you can take into consideration.

- Discuss the homework assignments with your student.
- Diverse kind of activities given and not only one pattern.
- Encourage your child to take notes on homework assignments when they are given.

- Give activities that boost children creativity; let them work in their happy zone.
- The time needed for homework should be studied, and each cycle should be considered a different stage.
- Parental involvement in the lesson should be considered. Lower grades usually need parents' involvement in a way or another and here we should be considering parent level of education.

Perhaps the most important advantage of homework is that it can increase achievement by extending learning beyond the school day. As parents, you all want to see your kids succeed, but as they search to find their footing on the pathway to success, it is important to help them show them that failure is part of the process, not an endpoint. And if you don't let them see you fail or experience a failure themselves in your presence, they may not have the stamina to overcome one when they are on their own. A better approach for giving homework is to ensure that teachers use homework effectively accomplished through a certain period of time.

Chapter 6
Emotional and Social Intelligence

"Anyone can become angry; that is easy. But to be angry with the right person to the right degree at the right time for the right purpose and in that right way—that is not easy."

– Aristotle

Most of us have emotional intelligence, but for most of us, it is an underdeveloped area. Academic and intellectual skills are very important, but they are not the only skills needed in the new age. Training our students to manage and control their emotions is as important as teaching them math, science, or any subject.

Emotions should be used as tools to succeed in our everyday lives. People who are emotionally intelligent can connect easily with people, lead, organize, and handle clashes that are bound to burst. They are natural leaders who know when to speak and when to stand up or bend to guide to achieve the goal.

Emotional and social intelligence is one important subject, just as MATH, English, etc., that should be taught in our schools since the early years. When emotional-social intelligence skills are a focus of learning, teachers and students are building human development behaviors that are related to the positive outcomes of achievement, goal achievement, and personal well-being.

Emotional learning is the knowledge and skills needed to identify and control feelings, whereas social learning covers the ethics and approaches that we need to collaborate effectively with others. Social-emotional learning involves emotional self-regulation and self-awareness, social knowledge and understanding, social skills, and social disposition.

1. Emotional intelligent leader

The school is not like any business; it cannot be divided, and the need to work all together is very important. A school should work tirelessly to shape its school culture to meet the needs of students and teachers. Collective intelligence is that when people work together, they create a kind of intelligence that just can't exist at an individual level. Thus, collective intelligence could be about creating harmony, making decisions together, brainstorming to come up with different ideas and questions, and even inspiring people through healthy levels of competition. So basically, the emotionally intelligent leader doesn't only depend on his mind but on the minds of all to get out of the best decision. A leader's intelligence has to have a strong emotional component. He /she has to have high levels of self-awareness, maturity, and self-control. He is also able to provide effective communication, listen effectively, and is open to positive and negative feedback. He applies collective leadership which means he considers his employees in his/her decisions.

Leaders with High Emotional Intelligence Are Able to:

- To understand the meaning of communicating effectively with all employees, tend to treat all employees with respect and empathy.
- To recognize the emotions that influence the attitudes and behaviors of employees.
- To express healthfully their emotions instead of allowing them to run wild.
- Take time to think before making any work-related decisions.
- View the problem from the point of view of others. Put himself/herself in others shoes and look through their eyes. It would be an excellent first step toward finding a common ground between two opposing points.
- Try to improve the five vital skills of emotional intelligence (self-awareness, self-regulation, internal motivation, social skills, and empathy).

2. **Social emotional intelligent teacher:**

Teachers play a great role in helping children respect differences and diversity at an early age, like gender, race, religion, and other characteristics. To become an emotionally intelligent teacher is a process and not an end result. As teachers, we should be working on ourselves to be role models, resilient to stress, and able to guide our students and orient them about different emotional and social intelligence skills. Teachers should be aware of social-emotional development in all its complication to prepare children to live in our changing world. Teachers, educators, mentors, or whatever we call them should be an instrument of inspiration instead of a tool of torture.

Researchers proved that teachers who purposely uses emotional skills and model emotionally intelligent behavior on a daily basis experience has more success and satisfaction in their professional careers and lives, as well as they are more optimistic and spreading positive vibes. Teachers have a great impact on students' way of thinking. Students are affected by teachers' emotional statues and they mostly do well when they are interested in the material and passionate about what they are learning.

Empathy is another factor of an emotionally intelligent teacher. It includes recognizing other people's feelings and then experiences their feeling. Researches show that students do better at school and get involved when the teacher shows them empathy and warmth, shows interest in their lives, and feels with them. Moreover, there is a correlation between students' emotional intelligence and their classroom behavior. Students with low emotional intelligence may not be able to build good relationships with their friends. They feel it is hard to communicate their feelings with their classmates and even adults.

Some expect children to learn skills of emotional intelligence indirectly from family dynamics and by participating in school and community activities. These skills include self-expression of emotions, conflict resolution, and empathy, which is, in other words, able to express one's thoughts and defend them, solve problems they face, and feel with others. Some consider it is something innate in people, but that is not always the case, as we can see in the scenarios mentioned in the first part of my book. We need actually to train our children to understand themselves better than others through classroom instruction, modeling, and even role-playing. The benefits of such skills are at two different levels:

- **A- At intrapersonal levels, students will know their feelings, control them, and have higher self-confidence.**
- **B- At interpersonal levels, students should learn to accept others, show compassion, kindness, and mercy, and being able to listen to others.**

The main pillar of quality education is the teacher. The teacher has the greatest impact on students during the school day; she/he plays several crucial roles to ensure that classroom strategies for improvement address the needs of students at all levels of learning and to develop approaches for improving the level of student achievement. Selecting a good teacher is not the only thing a school should do, but there are different steps that should be taken, which can be summarized as follows:

The selection of teacher: Choosing a teacher who deserves the title is hard and wrongly understood. It is not about the years of experience as most schools consider or a new generation (new blood, a new graduate). It is the result of a process that we talked about before. A teacher's job is not less important than a doctor's, and that's why she/he needs to be qualified to handle this job. A lifelong learning process and evaluation should be demanded.

Focused professional development: Empowering teachers and allowing them to be continuously learning through different ways is a must and not only a need. It is not about workshops on a yearly basis but on a weekly and daily basis. Teachers should be having homework other than correcting and preparing exams or lesson plans; a continuous process of development should be implemented through different strategies.

Cultural competence and culturally responsive: A teacher should develop a learning environment that is relevant to their students' social, cultural, and linguistic experiences. They act as guides, educators, consultants, and supporters for their students, helping to effectively connect their culturally and community-based knowledge to the classroom learning experience. As well as reshaping the curriculum in a way that allows culturally responsive teaching. It should be integrated, interdisciplinary, and student-centered. It should include issues and topics related to the student's background and culture.

Rewarding their work encourages teachers to be more creative and humanize their students. A teacher is a human being who needs to be treated with empathy and support as well through regarding and appreciating them.

3. Social emotional intelligent student:

Emotional social intelligence (ESI) is a strong indicator of academic performance, social skills, making positive decisions, and a general sense of well-being in students. Educators are not only tasked to teach students the academic standards of the curriculum but are also tasked with giving them an opportunity for the child to experience how to interact with peers. Classrooms provide our students the opportunity to work together collaboratively and maintain how students talk and interact with one another, which helps them internalize new information and shapes the way they think.

Students with a higher emotional intelligence (EI) are more likely to comply socially and manage their time conveniently as compared to those having a low EI, known to be more vulnerable to irregular and harmful behavior (Pau, et al., 2004). As a matter of fact, learners having a high emotional intelligence prove to be more obsolete, learn faster, behave ethically, and regulate their feelings (Ghosh and Gill (2003). Much of traditional education is directed toward isolating the learner from all social interaction and considering education as toward one-on-one relationship between the learner and the objective material to be learned. We should recognize the social aspect of learning and use conversation, interaction with others, and the application of knowledge as important aspects of learning. Throughout my career, I have been sensitive to the way many teachers commented about children who do not get involved in the lesson or misbehave; teachers will tell a parent that their child needs to 'participate more in class'. The teacher has a responsibility to adjust his/her attitude toward quiet children and shift his/her classroom dynamics to allow all children to express their emotions and show their character. Maybe then the introverted child would feel safer exploring his or her thoughts and sharing them with the class. Teachers should keep in mind that learning is caught and never taught and prepare themselves to be role models as a first step toward teaching emotion and social intelligence because students are always excited to emulate grownups and imitate the caring behaviors they see in their teachers as well as in their parents. Social-emotional students have these skills;

- Are able to understand stress and stress management, teachers should be teaching them techniques that help them break the habit of emotional reactivity.
- Have high self-esteem and confidence, which will increase their productivity and personal satisfaction.
- Are able to manage anxiety and improve performance under pressure. Students should learn how to challenge themselves and work under pressure without having anxiety.
- Are able to understand and accept differences in others and diversity issue. Students should not only end up successful but also human who can feel with others. They should learn to have empathy.
- Are decision makers, which is the ability to plan, express, and implement effective problem-solving criteria in worrying situations. Students should be able to take good decisions and become problem solvers.
- Are leaders by positively impacting, persuading, and influencing others? A leader is found in each and every one of us. The leader in me is one of

the topics that should be introduced by the teacher so that every student does a SWOT analysis about himself and tries to turn his weakness into a strength.
- Know the importance of time and be able to manage it to meet goals and assignments. Orienting students about the importance of time is one of the most important duties of a teacher.
- Have commitment ethics, which enable them to complete tasks and responsibilities in a timely and dependable manner.
- Are able to control and manage anger and improve performance under stressful conditions and situations.
- Have emotional honesty and self-regulation. Students should be able to express their ideas clearly and decently.
- Honor diversity and accepts differences. Students must have a positive self-identity and know that their gender, culture, and other traits are to be valued, as well as the cultures and traits of others.

What is Emotional and Psychological Trauma?

Students overwhelmed with exams and school work are experiencing an emotional and psychological trauma which is the result of extraordinarily stressful events that shatter their sense of security, making them feel helpless in a dangerous world. Other than that, some students come to school after experiencing a traumatic experience. The more frightened and helpless he/she feels, the more likely he/she is to be traumatized.

Emotional and psychological trauma can be caused by:

- One-time events, such as an accident, injury, or violent attack, especially if it was unexpected or happened in childhood.
- Ongoing, relentless stress, such as living in a crime-ridden neighborhood, battling a life-threatening illness, or experiencing traumatic events that occur repeatedly, such as bullying, domestic violence, or childhood neglect.
- Commonly overlooked causes, such as surgery (especially in the first three years of life), the sudden death of someone close, the breakup of a significant relationship, or a humiliating or deeply disappointing experience, especially if someone was deliberately cruel.

Teachers and leaders should be understanding and dig deep to understand the student's real agony. The most important part is to diagnose the problem before it become worse. Experiencing trauma in childhood can result in a severe and long-lasting effect.

Emotional and psychological Symptoms:	**Physical symptoms:**
• Shock, denial, or disbelief	• Insomnia or night mares
• Confusion, difficulty concentrating	• Fatigue
• Anger, irritability, mood swings, aggressive behavior	• Being startled easily
• Anxiety and fear	• Difficulty concentrating
• Guilt, shame, and self-blame	• Racing heartbeat
• Withdrawing from others	• Edginess and
• Feeling sad or hopeless	• Aches and pains
• Feeling disconnected	• Muscle tension

How teachers should deal with traumatized students is the most important part of this topic because here the teachers play the role of the doctor, who has to search and seek help from the specialist or a trained health professional so that she can really help the child. These students are not stupid or do poorly because they lack intelligence but they have experienced hard situations that have made them tend to be tedious, have trouble following the rules, and appear to be disruptive. They seem to have trouble concentrating and may spend their time daydreaming. We should be careful that failure in school and criticism from teachers, parents, or classmates often leave these students frustrated and worthless. As teachers, we should participate in building gritty students.

"A person who never made a mistake never tried something new."

Albert Einstein

Who is a Gritty student?

A gritty student has a growth mindset; when bad things happen, he does not give up and dares to continue. He/she acknowledges his or her feelings about the trauma as they arise and accepts them. While it is important for our students to succeed, they also need to learn how to manage failure. They should be able to see failure as a first step to success and not an end. A kid who is always an "A" student will see the "B" as an end. They will struggle to pick themselves up again when they experience their first real failure. They grow up to be "fragile perfects."

Fragile perfects are defenseless high achievers who know how to succeed but not how to fail. And that's the problem. Everyone will experience failure at some point in his/her lives. They need to know how to bounce back from it. The longer it takes for this first failure to happen, the harder it is to learn how to bounce back. That's often what happens with "fragile perfects" by the time they get their first failure, they've been on a winning streak for such a long time that it can be devastating.

One of the difficulties with introducing failure is doing it in a way that is natural. We don't want to force our children into an impossible situation just to make sure that they get the experience of failing. However, they do need to experience the occasional setback that will help them build resilience for future obstacles.

Schools should dedicate more intentional effort to developing grit in students. Teaching grit means helping students understand how to set and achieve their goals. When we teach students how to regulate their attention, emotions, and behavior, we empower them to pursue goals. At one time or another, we all have been impressed by an athlete, a student, or a musician whom we would label as 'talented'. Talent, however, is only part of the picture. When students struggle with a task, they may believe that they lack the ability to solve the problem and, therefore, give up. It is important for students to understand that it is OK to feel confused when learning something new, and actually, it is expected. We can teach students that making mistakes or taking a long time to complete an assignment is a normal part of learning, not a sign of failure. Grit involves working enthusiastically toward challenges, maintaining effort and interest over years despite failure, hardship, and plateaus in progress. The gritty individual approaches achievement as a marathon; his or her advantage is stamina. Gritty people don't change their paths because of disappointment or lose hope and feel boredom.

We can all identify people in our lives who have big ideas and a lot of enthusiasm for many projects, only to drop them within a few weeks. Individuals with a lot of grit tend to set very long-term objectives and do not lose sight of them, even when they are not getting any positive feedback.

Grit is teachable, although at the same time, teaching a student "passion and perseverance toward long-term goals" sounds like a difficult task but can be achieved if the teacher herself is a gritty person. She/he can start by consistently repeating the following activities:

Help the student have dreams, goals, and a core purpose in life.

Encourage him/her to conduct "grit interviews" of adults in his life.

Teach students about grit through stories of famous people who failed before finding success.

Read stories about grit and help students connect them to their own lives.

When he wants to give up, always ask him about the hard part and help him solve it.

Share your own passions with your students, and pursue them regularly.

These simple activities can help your students build the passion and perseverance they need to succeed in school and in life.

Teaching Optimism: Optimism is a skill that can be taught by changing how we view the holdups we meet in life. Parents and teachers are supposed to model and teach these skills because children learn either pessimism or optimism from the adults in their lives.

Working with Emotions: Teach students how to work with their emotions. Just changing their thoughts is sometimes not enough for students, particularly if they tend to get anxious, appear depressed, or come from a different environment. Their emotions should not hijack them. I know to talk about emotions seems unpretentious but it is not as it seems for all of the student. We all have different mindsets, but we should train our children to see the good in everything. None can destroy iron, but its own rust can. Likewise, no one can destroy a person but his own MINDSET can. Emotion researchers have found cognitive reappraisal to be the ideal method to adjust difficult emotions. Some students suppress their emotions as a way to regulate them. Teachers need to be aware of students who might be doing this, gritty or not. Emotional suppression means just that: pushing away rather than dealing with difficult thoughts and emotions. Students should learn how to deal with their emotions and regulate them.

Building Resilience: Resilience is related to grit because part of what it means to be gritty is to be resilient when challenges present themselves. There are many other traits a student must possess in order to be gritty, which include carefulness, self-discipline, and persistence. Students who nurture positive emotions are able to bounce back from obstacles and the negative emotions that often follow.

Deepening Self-Awareness: The unseen benefits of teaching these 'grit skills' is that students will also gain a better understanding of who they are as human beings. And hopefully along the way, they will develop more empathy and compassion for those around them who may be struggling to reach a goal, making everyone a winner in the end. In this age, companies are not only demanding people with brains but also people with hearts who are able to show love for their company and who are real human beings. They can understand others and work with them for the sake of the success of all. Finally, if we accept that social and emotional learning should be an important part of the curriculum, we must identify and train ourselves to implement the teaching strategies that encourage it. First and foremost, we must recognize that social-emotional learning is a content area just like literacy, mathematics, and other disciplines. At the end, we all want the same things for ourselves, our leaders, and our communities to live peacefully, to accept others for who they are and value their feelings, thoughts, and actions, and to create relationships characterized by mutual respect and trust. An early recognition of the importance of social emotional development in our lives can achieve these individual and collective goals. The school should build its learning program knowing that the child has to be free from fear before anything else can be achieved—free from the fear of failure, the fear of being themselves, and the fear of the learning process. Kids have an endless energy and the motivation to be the change the world needs. We as teachers should believe that learning is impactful when it is real.

Chapter 7
Different Hats a Teacher Should Wear

Bamboo Curriculum Needs A Bamboo Teacher

The Lesson of Bamboo

We are all familiar with Bamboo plant. Bamboo tree is a symbol of strength, flexibility, renewal, growth, and it can also mean having good health and luck in your life. You can learn from the Bamboo plant that you need to adapt to situations and must be able to use your strength for something of excellence. A Bamboo teacher has a character made of bamboo which means that you need to be both lenient and tough. A bamboo is tolerant and show it through being more considerate to others. **Bamboo teacher you must be!**

This largest member of the grass family has a unique growth pattern. It seems to the unexperienced eye that a recently planted bamboo appears to be doing nothing, as there is no visible growth above ground after year one, year two or year three. However, the roots of the plant are busy just like the bee to develop, gather nutrients to appear with new growth. This growth pattern of the Bamboo is similar to the success of a teacher. Time for the bamboo to grow is measured in years and is unspectacular and unseen. A BAMBOO plant needs time to grow and to have this beautiful shape in the end. It teaches us patience. Similarly, it takes time for the teacher to see the results of his/her hard work. As we all know we cannot sow and reap at the same time. Teachers should be like Bamboo plants able to adjust and flexible to meet the needs of work keeping in mind that good things take time Similarly, Nelson Mandela said in his biograph The Long Walk, to Freedom, "In some ways, I saw the garden as a metaphor for certain aspects of my life. A teacher must also tend his garden; he, too, plants seeds and then watches, cultivates, and harvests the result. Like the gardener, a leader must take responsibility for what he cultivates; he must mind his work, try to repel enemies, preserve what can be preserved, and eliminate what cannot succeed." In this part of the book, you will get to know the different hats that a school teacher should wear in order to be a Bamboo teacher.

Emotionally Intelligent Teacher

The Red Hat

Teachers have a great role in creating a difference in school and student performance if they are given independence to make important decisions. However, autonomy alone does not lead to improvements unless it is well supported. Teachers need appropriate support that allows them to focus on the practices that lead to the improvement of student learning and building their characters. This autonomy should be coupled with new models of distributed leadership, new types of accountabilities, and training to develop teacher quality, to increase congeniality between teachers and teamwork, as well as goal-setting, assessment, and accountability. A teacher should have emotional intelligence elements as stated by Daniel Goleman, including empathy, relationship management, self-awareness, self-management, and motivation.

Emotionally Intelligent Teacher

Emotional intelligence is a must for a school teacher willing to move forward and to succeed in building trust and creating a culture where teaching and learning flourish.

Emotional intelligence is considered to be the ability to join emotion and rationality, using emotions to understand reasoning and wisely think about it. The aim of a teacher is to humbly teach students and guide them toward a better future and to a better version of themselves. It doesn't mean to be always able to deal with his emotions and to maintain an emotional balance without going over the edge. We always wish that we shouldn't get dominated by our emotions, or else we will take irrational decisions and we may be losing if we didn't learn to tolerate, and this is what a teacher should do and teach her students to do so.

When I say EI, I don't mean there is no need for IQ, but we live in a world now where a smart person nowadays is considered a genius before. The world has developed, and many new problems have appeared, from poverty to environmental destruction to diseases and natural disasters. We need more problem solvers and people who are more human. Today's problems necessitate not only IQ but also EQ. We cannot deny that IQ is an important element of success, but it is also recognized that it is not the only determinant of life success. Schools now focus more on developing critical thinkers, communicators, collaborators, and students with high emotional intelligence more than students. The aim of school changed from teaching knowledge to building a healthy person with a great ability to communicate and make a difference. Knowledge is not the only aim anymore because students have access to knowledge at any time, but to build students' characters and to allow them to be more human. Schools aim to teach multiple intelligences, which include offering character education, modeling positive behaviors, encouraging students to think about how others are feeling, and finding ways to be more empathetic toward others.

The term empathy is explained by being able to put ourselves in somebody shoes and to walk a mile in their shoes, which is the ability to understand what others feel and think. Empathy is important because it helps teachers to deal with students with different backgrounds, environments, religions, and conditions. With these semantics in mind, we offer the idea of an "empathetic teacher" as someone who seeks to both understand a student's condition from their perspective and understand the needs of others, with the aim of acting to make a difference in responding to those needs or building on the positives. In other words, the goal is to humanize the work by having the ability to emotionally understand what students feel, see things from their point of view, and imagine yourself in their place. The aim of the teacher should be to create a culture of trust and joy before teaching.

A teacher functions much like a parent in building a young person's brain. A caring teacher who shows positive regard for a learner, demonstrates optimism, is encouraging, and minimizes classroom conflict positively impacts student achievement (Cozolino, 2013). In addition, Carol Dweck's work (2006) makes a compelling case for the importance of teachers working from a growth mindset about their students so those students can develop a growth mindset about themselves and others.

A school environment has a great role in creating such a teacher through developing an inclusive place with democracy aspirations where community functions as it should be. Teachers in such an environment where dialogue exists and not just monologue gives students voices to be part of everything what to learn, how and what to examine. Children are not in schools to achieve mastery on achievement tests but to learn to have sympathy and compassion, to be more human, and able to lead themselves firstly to a better place without hurting others but through supporting others.

An emotionally intelligent teacher is able to recognize his emotions, understand them, and manage them to suit a goal or situation. After this pandemic we had faced, we really understood that schooling is one of the most important things in life, just like health and food. The teaching revolution allowed us to think differently about schools and teaching. The need to have empathy and compassion is really regarded. Leaders of schools have a great role in developing good teachers through their leadership skills. Things that leaders should focus on include listening more, solving problems, showing empathy to others in need, being more present and focused, empowering rather than micromanaging others, managing frustration or disappointment more effectively, and being more in tune with the emotions of those around them rather than making assumptions.

Servant Teacher

The Green Hat

Servant teacher is a teacher that has an aim to serve. A servant teacher shares power, consider the needs of the students first and empower people to develop and improve.

The servant teacher assumes that the most effective teaches are servants of their people. There is no hierarchy, it put emphasis on trust, empathy, and ethics. Servant teachers should remember these ten characteristics: listening, empathy, healing, awareness, persuasion, conceptualization, foresight, stewardship, commitment to the growth of others, and building community. The servant teacher aims to create a healthy environment that allows positive relationships. Servant teachers are able to put together a diverse group of students from all walks of life, respecting their ideas and encouraging them to try new approaches to improve work and value them.

Authorities style versus lenient style case study:
Is it Better to be Loved or Feared?
The Case for Fear

An authoritarian approach also has advantages. Some students may take advantage of teachers who use a lenient way, that's why in certain situations a teacher has to be strict but not too intimidating. They can use "tough love" to "whip students into shape." Authoritarian teachers make those boundaries clear through showing the results for not adhering to rules. Real respect must be earned and involves respecting others and caring about students. Students might tend to flare up when a teacher approach student from an authoritarian standpoint.

However, the teacher's success is not based on being more loved or being feared more. Both have their upsides, but each also has its downside. Beloved teachers might be popular, but they might also be easily manipulated and put into unnecessary situations. This means that the lenient style should have a certain stop when limits are exceeded. The training is a must to teach this style and redeem the cases to have a middle ground.

The Middle Ground

Respect is a two-way street and must be earned. Both styles have upsides and downsides; perhaps the best approach is to do a little bit of both. Like an authoritative teacher, you want to have clear boundaries with clear consequences, but you do not want to create a fearful and poisonous class where everyone is trying to stab each other in the back and no one will tell you the truth but whatever you want to hear. In addition, a middle-ground approach would mean that you do value your students and you are genuinely interested in their talents and silly stories. Yet, imposing clear boundaries is a must. Your job includes pressure, and there is no one size that fits all. The key to understanding whether it is better to be loved or feared is considering the big picture and the long term and, in each situation, determining which approach would be more effective in the long run for that situation. A middle-ground approach is a convincing one in most cases. The teacher should be capable of changing his style at the right time and in the right situation. Personally, I do not believe in typecasting a style as "lenient" or "strict." Any teacher may say that his or her style is ideal. Sometimes, you will stumble upon such teachers like this by blind luck.

How to become the most approachable teacher using your emotional intelligence?

Being an approachable teacher starts with getting rid of the boss moniker altogether. This may be the most intelligent decision you ever make as a teacher, and it will be the beginning of your transformation from teacher to leader. People work harder when they love the work and the place they are in; they work harder with the people who inspire them and support them. Put in mind that you want to serve and support your students in their learning journey. To be approachable, you should have a servant mindset and to be able to control your moods that are infectious in most of the times.

Servant teachers work for their students, not for themselves. Nelson Mandela and Mahatma Gandhi are recognizable examples of servant teachers in practice. Servant teachers are emotionally intelligent. They are expert communicators, sympathetic collaborators, and apply moral authority. The servant teachers need emotional intelligence to view their role to empower others to become better at what they do and to be able to serve others by moral authority, humility, service, and sacrifice in order to create trust, foster teamwork, and achieve vision of the school.

Moral Leadership

The White Hat

A moral teacher should be willing to serve, serving those around one and subordinating oneself to the vision and best interests of the organization. A moral teacher considers values, attitudes, and morals as part of decision-making. The heart, mind, and body of a moral teacher work together to make decisions. A heart should be involved, and this heart should be filled with the three components of empathy, sympathy, and compassion.

Moral intelligence and emotional intelligence are two types of intelligence that make you different. Moral intelligence is our mental capacity should apply the universal human qualities such as integrity, responsibility, compassion, and forgiveness to our personal values, goals, and actions.

Integrity is the substance of a successful relationship and the capstone of moral intelligent teacher. It is having strong ethical and moral principles that creates trust and a professional culture in which people can depend on one another and treat each other with respect.

Responsibility is another key quality of a morally intelligent person. Only a person willing to take responsibility for his actions—and the consequences of those actions—will be able to be trusted and worked with in the sense that they don't run away and blame others.

Compassion is important because it communicates our respect for others.

Forgiveness is a crucial principle because, without TOLERATING mistakes and learning from them, we are likely to be rigid, inflexible, and unable to engage with others in ways that promote our mutual good.

Relation Between Emotional Intelligence and Moral Intelligence

Emotional intelligence can help you behave with great self-control and interpersonal understanding. But it won't keep you from doing the wrong thing unless you have morals and core values.

Although both emotional intelligence and moral intelligence come into play when moral decisions are at stake, they are not the same. Teachers can be charismatic and influential in a deeply destructive way without morality and the knowledge of these morals in our everyday lives. Moral intelligence is the "central intelligence" for all humans. It is what gives our lives meaning.

Moral intelligence is a renewable asset that needs to be developed and renewed, which will give you singular personal satisfaction and professional rewards. Using your morals and staying true to your moral compass will not remove life's inevitable conflicts and will not mean you will not make mistakes, but you will solve these issues positively and have a sense of personal wellbeing. It is like the global positioning system that is used in cars and that allows you to better harness all the resources of your life. It is basic equipment for individuals who want to reach their best creative potential.

Teachers who are morally gifted do less mistakes than others; they all do mistakes more often, but they learn from them and move on. They take responsibility of their failures and held themselves responsible for their moral lapses. Their reaction to the mistake is what counts and not the mistakes themselves. If you pay attention to your own moral intelligence and encourage the development of moral intelligence throughout your organization, you inspire the best efforts of everyone—and your performance will outpace your competitors. The questions that a teacher should keep in mind are: 'What does it mean to educate someone?' and 'How do we recognize an educated person?' These are profound questions that will shape our understanding of schools, the curriculum, the roles of teachers and students, and the nature of educational leadership.

Morals are morals and cannot be outdated or should be updated. Moral teachers ask the students to be moral and lead by example, brave and fair, guide and direct people to be the moral icons of their society, a person of trust responsible, accountable, gifted with honesty and integrity, and above all having compassion toward the people working with him. There is no update for morality; it is beyond times, seasons, geographical horizons, and people; it is the same in all religions; what is wrong is wrong, with no need to be proved. A moral teacher is mindfully humble in his or her mindset and accepts their mistakes by putting their egos aside to open their mind to new possibilities. They are able to take risks and are not afraid of failure because they believe that, all together, they can overcome any obstacle. Other than being a role model and challenging others to be more human and supportive, they live for others in a way that they consider their position is for the sake of the people they lead and the community they are in, and this is done by cultivating empathy and compassion.

Morals is a common language no matter what lens a person one is using. It is a central matter of our existence. The core of teaching includes four basic values: dignity, truthfulness, fairness, and responsibility and freedom.

Respect summarizes all these skills; a teacher should respect all students and listens to them in a way to treat them as he or she treats herself.

"The essential thing is not knowledge but character," said Joseph Le Conte.

The significance of the impact educators has on shaping the impressionable young minds of students is more than the most detailed lesson plans or the prescription of a curriculum map. The teachable moments an educator injects into the moral fiber of students are the lessons that become a ripple that impacts others for a lifetime.

Yet, in a society that values standardized test scores over character education, quickly eliminating the social interactions that build integrity for hours spent with artificial intelligence is creating a culture that idolizes a filtered social media post over giving an undocumented hand to those in need. The power of our actions and investment in the moral and ethical education of students will pay dividends because you create more than knowledge; you arm students with the power of goodness and **kindness**, which far supersede any other score.

Why Does Teaching Morality Matter?

Turn on the evening news, and the reason for incorporating character education reaches out and grabs us like a bad dream. The daily dose of reported violence, apathy, offense, and divisiveness has desensitized us to the deterioration of moral character. Teaching morality matters because treating your neighbor as yourself has become a less and less frequent practice. We need a little less TikTok and a little more Mr. Rogers. Schools have the platform to instill what has been missing in our curriculum for so long, but how do we do it?

How to Connect Morality to Academics

Like so many best practices that have been ingrained in educators, morality does not have to be taught in isolation but can be partnered with content to make learning experiences impactful in more ways than one.

Be a Role Model

Teachers are heroes in the eyes of their students. What makes you stand out even more is to practice what you preach. Just like a great teacher models thinking strategies, demonstrating for students how to show moral character is just as important.

On several occasions, I have seen a teacher apologize for a wrongdoing toward a child. Saying "I'm sorry," can be difficult, especially when it is never seen at home. The freedom that comes with recognizing we made a mistake, owning it, and asking for forgiveness is a priceless gift we can share with our students.

Teachers are role models every day when they show compassion, sharing, choosing kind words when it would be easier to shout, and advocating for the marginalized populations. Never underestimate the difference you can make when you leave your signature on a student's mindset.

Connect to Your Content

The autonomy in teaching manifests itself oftentimes in the details. Choosing examples or opportunities for your students to intertwine content with principled foundations proves impactful for students.

At my school, Washington County Elementary School, we ask teachers to involve students in a **passion project**. Students were learning about animals in a kindergarten/first grade split classroom, and as a result, the students chose to adopt an animal clinic. The students brought in pet food and supplies and donated them. In turn, they learned about the life cycles of animals that visit the clinic. They wrote cards to the vets, thanking them for their service. They added together the supplies and the cost of the supplies to incorporate math skills. The teacher chose guided reading books and interactive read-aloud texts that focused on animal life cycles.

The experience was rich for students, and their enthusiasm for the work they were doing showed through their pride in their work. All students were engaged and wanted to explain to me all about the project they were doing, and I was always beaming when they used such sophisticated vocabulary to paint a vivid picture for me, one I never get about a worksheet!

Encourage Positive Behaviors

Providing reinforcement of positive behaviors, as opposed to positively reinforcing negative behaviors, keeps your classroom in a state of growth. Pouring all of your energy into the negative leaves educators drained with no real results. Rather than focusing on what is not going well, praise the positive. When students make a mistake, do not ignore it; instead, allow them to grow through it. This makes your classroom a safe place, and students will have the innate desire to please.

Building Grit

One of the golden opportunities teachers often allow to pass them by is when a student makes a mistake and we do not take the time to **reflect upon how the mistake was an open door for learning**. As a result, we have a generation of students who are terrified to be anything less than perfect. In the hallways, PLCs, faculty meetings, and parent-teacher conferences, I constantly hear how kids are not motivated, but in return, what I want to say is that we have not taught nor expected grit from students today. It is significant to teach students to press through difficult tasks. When a student does not meet the expectation, whether it be behavioral or academic, take the time to allow students to correct mistakes.

Years ago, as a young, eager student, I would have told you that a great teacher was someone who provided classroom entertainment and gave very little homework. Needless to say, after many years of K-12 administrative experience and giving hundreds of teacher evaluations, my perspective has changed. My current position as a professor in higher education gives me the opportunity to share what I have learned with current and future school leaders and allows for some lively discussions among my graduate students in terms of what it means to be a great teacher.

Teaching is hard work, and some teachers never grow to be anything better than mediocre. They do the bare minimum required and very little more. The great teachers, however, work tirelessly to create a challenging, nurturing environment for their students. Great teaching seems to have less to do with our knowledge and skills than with our attitude toward our students, our subject, and our work. Although this list is certainly not all-inclusive, I have narrowed down the many characteristics of a great teacher to those I have found to be the most essential, regardless of the age of the learner:

1. **A great teacher respects students.** In a great teacher's classroom, each person's ideas and opinions are valued. Students feel safe expressing their feelings and learn to respect and listen to others. This teacher creates a welcoming learning environment for all students.
2. **A great teacher creates a sense of community and belonging in the classroom.** The mutual respect in this teacher's classroom provides a supportive, collaborative environment. In this small community, there are rules to follow and jobs to be done, and each student is aware that he or she is an important, integral part of the group. A great teacher lets students know that they can depend not only on her but also on the entire class.
3. **A great teacher is warm, accessible, enthusiastic, and caring.** This person is approachable, not only to students but to everyone on campus. This is the teacher to whom students know they can go with any problems or concerns—or even to share a funny story. Great teachers possess good listening skills and take time out of their way-too-busy schedules for anyone who needs them. If this teacher is having a bad day, no one ever knows—the teacher leaves personal baggage outside the school doors.
4. **A great teacher sets high expectations for all students.** This teacher realizes that the expectations she has for her students greatly affect their

achievement; she knows that students generally give to teachers as much or as little as is expected of them.
5. **A great teacher has his own love of learning** and inspires students with his passion for education and for the course material. He constantly renews himself as a professional on his quest to provide students with the highest quality education possible. This teacher has no fear of learning new teaching strategies or incorporating new technologies into lessons and always seems to be the one who is willing to share what he's learned with colleagues.
6. **A great teacher is a skilled leader.** Different from administrative leaders, effective teachers focus on shared decision-making and teamwork, as well as on community building. This great teacher conveys this sense of leadership to students by providing opportunities for each of them to assume leadership roles.
7. **A great teacher can "shift-gears"** and is flexible when a lesson isn't working. This teacher assesses his teaching throughout the lessons and finds new ways to present material to make sure that every student understands the key concepts.
8. **A great teacher collaborates with colleagues on an ongoing basis.** Rather than thinking of herself as weak because she asks for suggestions or help, this teacher views collaboration as a way to learn from a fellow professional. A great teacher uses constructive criticism and advice as an opportunity to grow as an educator.
9. **A great teacher maintains professionalism in all areas,** from personal appearance to organizational

skills and preparedness for each day. Her communication skills are exemplary, whether she is speaking with an administrator, one of her students, or a colleague. The respect that the great teacher receives because of her professional manner is obvious to those around her.

While teaching is a gift that seems to come quite naturally for some, others have to work overtime to achieve great teacher status. Yet the payoff is enormous—for both you and your students. Imagine students thinking of you when they remember that great teacher they had in college!

Dr. Maria Orlando is a core faculty member in the doctoral Educational Leadership and Management Specialization at Capella University. She also serves as an adjunct professor at Lindenwood University in St. Charles, Missouri.

How to Develop Cultural Leadership

Cultural Intelligence of a School Leader

The black hat

Cultural intelligence is the ability to accept others cultures and differences and the impact on their behaviors, and how effectively the organization engages in different environmental settings. There are three aspects in which cultural intelligence arises: cognitive, physical, and through motivational means. These traits allow an individual to acquire a high sense of cultural intelligence in the context that is needed. In order to understand others, we need to understand their cultures by studying the beliefs, customs, and norms of other cultures. A teacher needs to become more knowledgeable of other cultures by studying the beliefs, customs, and norms of foreign culture. Culturally intelligent teachers understand that it takes time for a new culture to be considered uniform. Teamwork is a way to have a melting pot in your organization, and team participants must be proactive and seek to obtain synergy before conflicts occur and allow teamwork to occur. They don't only accept the differences but are also interested in knowing more about other cultures and learning more about them to become more effective and respectful in any cultural situation. They are able to tolerate Tolerance and leadership are relevant. After all, we want to have a new way of thinking and think outside the box; that's why we should teach people to accept others' opinions and who are able to work in a team full of diverse cultures.

The black hat is actually the hat of the architect, who has to design his thinking to face the different cultures and design the school model. Design thinking is a problem-solving approach, which is concerned with identifying the problem and spotting the factors that led to this problem. The first step to design thinking is to question everything you see in an attempt to find new approaches and solutions that are new and reliable. Design thinking is considered thinking outside the box and an effort to develop new ways of thinking that are new and innovative. It enables us to improve our experience by being culturally responsive teachers.

Any culturally responsive teacher should have emotional intelligence to be able to negotiate across cultures and interpret the actions of a different culture, and work more effectively across cultures. Cultural teachers are able to face cross-cultural challenges using their emotional intelligence to know others and themselves as well. A teacher can work on his cultural intelligence and make it better and boost his cross-cultural knowledge by reading, studying, and learning about the ways' cultures vary and how cultures compare to each other. But remember that knowledge alone is not enough. A teacher has to find a common ground between his culture and the culture of others and by dropping the golden thought that his culture is better than others. Teachers should not only be aware of others cultures but to promote opportunities for cultural and creative learning within their classes.

Digital Leadership

Digital Age

Digital natives are those who have been in the digital age and technology is part of their life. They are able to exist, operate, and lead in this world prior to the integration of technology. There is a clear failure in education due to the needs of leaders and educators to understand the needs of modern students. It is too hard for students of this age to excel using outdated teaching methods. Being digitally intelligent as a leader is part of success in this age.

Digital intelligence includes the understanding of the importance of technology in our lives, including strength, opportunities, and advantages, by knowing types of it with its different applications that makes things easier and well developed. Today, the hurrying of technological innovations has transformed the use, behaviors, and practices of leaders as well as the responsibilities of schools, which will be to help students develop their digital intelligence so they can adapt easily to changes and cope with potential threats. This ability to acquire and apply new knowledge and skills related to digital technologies is called digital intelligence.

This digital intelligence, which is a need in this age, includes creating a digital identity and maintaining a good e-reputation, effectively and appropriately using social media. As work becomes increasingly dominated by technology, we need new ways of thinking to continue to be effective. Our ability to acquire and apply new knowledge and skills is what we call intelligence.

Digital intelligence is not about the use of digital tools at the exclusion of human ability, but rather it is about the relative strengths of both people and technology and playing to those strengths. It is built by using different kinds of intelligence.

Digital Literacy

Literacy is no longer about reading and writing skills. "Digital literacy is the ability to use information and communication technologies to find, evaluate, create, and communicate information, requiring both cognitive and technical skills." It includes the ability to use and create digital content as well as communicate it. Teachers of the digital age need to try and tap into the full potential of the people who work for them, which means they have to have a greater understanding of what their people can do, empower them more, and also ask more questions. Now teachers are sometimes struggling with new technologies, and their success depends on their willingness to learn something new and keep things simple to cut out wasted effort. In other words, they are curious to know more about technologies because they are also interested and have made their work easier and more creative.

Final Thought

We are digital natives living in a world where with a touch or swipe of a pocket-sized screen, we can instantly communicate with anyone, anywhere; find whatever information we need; and buy any product we want. That's why nobody can isolate himself or herself from the world, and even our markets are full of products from different regions of the world. We have lived through natural disasters, and we are facing unpredictable challenges. It is described as volatile, uncertain, complex, and ambiguous. As teachers, we should keep in mind a few questions, like: What will our world look like when our youngest students graduate? Will they feel secure and be able to survive conflicts between nations and ethnic groups that are declining while technology is being harnessed to protect the planet's environment and natural resources? Nobody knows what will the new jobs, leaders, or organization that will survive. The big question remains as: What docs all of this have to do with schools and school leaders?

The answer is simply everything. School is the place to change everything, change of mindsets in the first place. It is the only place that allows students to be global citizens of this mother earth and learn to love it. The exact goals of school in this age will be a way to prepare youth for democratic citizenship, bolster economic growth by creating a knowledgeable and well-trained workforce, and prepare students for a new world and support them with skills for the new workforce like critical thinking, collaboration, and creativity. Thus, we need to make education more relevant.

I tried to clarify throughout this part of the book that a teacher should have different intelligences other than logical reasoning and technical knowledge, and there is a great responsibility toward investing in our leaders to strengthen their intelligence competencies by allowing them to develop and master self-awareness. In our global and modern world, it no longer solely matters if a person received the best education or training from the best institution. An intelligent and rational teacher with a high IQ is a great asset, but it does not stand as the most important qualification. A teacher who has developed their skills in other intelligence competencies such as emotional intelligence, cultural intelligence, moral intelligence, digital intelligence, gender intelligence, and global intelligence (to name a few) is likely to succeed in this career in this age.